C000004772

DESIGNING CHANGE

DESIGNING CHANGE

THE ART OF COIN DESIGN

Edited by Kevin Clancy

A Royal Mint publication

First published in Great Britain in 2008
Published by the Royal Mint
Llantrisant, Pontyclun CF72 8YT
United Kingdom

www.royalmint.com

Images copyright as attributed

ISBN 978-1-869917-06-7

A CIP catalogue record for this book is available from the British Library

Designed by Tuch, London

Printed in the United Kingdom by Gavin Martin Associates Ltd, London

This book is published to coincide
with the exhibition at the British Museum
Designing Change: Coins of Elizabeth II
September 2008 to February 2009

The
Royal
Mint

Foreword

His Royal Highness
The Duke of Edinburgh

The invitation from the Prime Minister – Sir Winston Churchill – to become President of the Royal Mint Advisory Committee came from out of the blue, and it took me some time to discover just what it entailed. The invitation reached me only a few months before the Queen's Coronation, so that I was immediately confronted with the need to chair the Committee to organise the design of a completely new set of coins for the new reign. It was quite a challenge, but we must have got it right. I stayed on as President until 1999.

Needless to say, I knew absolutely nothing about the design of coins or of numismatic history, but the Committee was packed with experts, and all I had to do was to get them to agree. There was the rub! Getting a dozen experts from almost as many different fields to agree on a set of designs turned out to be a real, but wholly fascinating, challenge.

I very soon learned that the design of coins is a special art. It is not quite graphic, in that the face of the coin is not quite flat, and it is not quite sculptural in that it only has limited depth. Furthermore, the shape of most coins is round, so that a traditional rectangular 'picture' design does not work. I also discovered that the process of pressing the coins entails moving the metal so as to fill the moulds. This means that the design of one side of the coin has an influence on the other. If two low points coincide, the balance of metal is upset, and unwanted 'shadows' can appear. If the two sides of a coin are designed by different people, adjustment can cause difficulties! It is complicated even further when a third person is given the task of designing the lettering. Finally, it has to be suitable for its function.

The whole process of commissioning coins and their designs rests with the Royal Mint. The Committee, as its title implies, is purely advisory. In effect, it justifies the Royal Mint in its process of commissioning designers, and in the delicate business of discussing draft designs with the chosen artists. It is much easier for the Deputy Master of the Royal Mint to criticise designs produced by artists if he can say that he is passing on the comments of the Committee.

Of course, the ultimate authority for the issue of coinage, after the Sovereign, is the Chancellor of the Exchequer in his capacity as Master of the Royal Mint. This was normally not a problem, although there was one notable occasion when a Master disagreed with the selection proposed by the Committee. I am glad to say that the matter was resolved amicably.

I warmly welcome this book. Although the use of coins is general, and dates back many hundreds of years, the design of coins has remained rather an obscure art form. I hope this book will help interested readers to appreciate the intricacies of the art, and to follow the way it has developed over the centuries to achieve a practical purpose while, at the same time, reflecting contemporary tastes and attitudes.

8

A frank and open relationship: heraldry and coinage in British history

Clive Cheesman

Heraldry and coinage have long been intimately related in Britain, as indeed in all the countries of Europe. But not only did this intimacy take a surprisingly long time to develop, the relationship has always been very much an 'open' one. The coinage has frequently dallied with other forms of decorative design, and when it has taken up with heraldry the degree of its commitment and the practicalities of the partnership have varied greatly. It has always felt able to submit heraldry to a frank analysis. Nor has there ever been anything automatic or obvious about the choice to represent the Royal Arms on the coinage: it has been, for centuries, one of the leading options available, time and time again resorted to in order to produce distinctive and bold coinage; but not one that is characteristic of any particular age in British history.

Heraldry seems to have developed as a consistent system from the mid-twelfth century onwards. The kings of England had a stable coat of arms from 1198 at the latest and those of Scotland from about a generation later. But it is not until the fourteenth century that we find true heraldry on coins in the British Isles. This is surprising because much of our earliest evidence for the growth of heraldry comes from seals – like coins, small, round things combining words and images for easy recognition. The design and manufacture of a coin die was not unlike that of a seal matrix, though the one stamped metal and the other only wax; in later centuries, at least, the same designers and craftsmen have often worked on both.

There are some possible hints of heraldry, it is true. Some scholars have purported to see proto-heraldic symbols on the eleventh-century coinage of Flanders and elsewhere in northern Europe. Coins of Robert, Earl of Gloucester (illegitimate son of Henry I (1100-35) and half-brother of Matilda) have recently been discovered which seem to show the development of the distinctive walking, head-turned lion of English heraldry – the *lion passant guardant*, or 'leopard'. These suggestions of developing heraldic design are not, however, shown on shields; they are placed directly in the field of the coin and cannot therefore be taken as certain evidence of a stable coat of arms.

There is, in the loosest sense, something heraldically simple and geometric in the interplay of crosses and pellets and quatrefoil-shaped cartouches seen on the three great silver coinages of the twelfth and thirteenth centuries. But this is a characteristic shared by much medieval design and decoration. The same can be said of the Scottish pennies of the same period, with their crosses and stars; and while King John (1199-1216) may have been using the English lions on his shield and his seal before and after accession, they are quite absent from the coins he issued in Dublin as Lord of Ireland.

Partly this was a result of conservatism and centralised control of minting, deriving in turn from the relative stability of the English coinage and the desire to stick to a reputable brand. In the feudal states of twelfth-century Germany the silver coinage was a product in serious decline, continually minted in smaller or thinner form, or just in baser metal; the frequent recall of the coins for reminting with new types resulted in a great array of interesting designs, with fabulous beasts and elaborate borders often giving the coins an heraldic look. In other parts of Europe where minting was in the hands of local potentates, coinage similarly turned into a vehicle for competitive self-advertisement. In the thirteenth century, with the development of the silver multiple known as the *gros* in French (*grosso* in Italian, *groschen* in German) and the revival of gold coinages, there were simply more platforms for heraldic and quasi-heraldic imagery.

When English mints started minting silver multiples (known as groats) under Edward I (1272-1307), heraldry remained absent. But it burst into life on the gold coinage produced under his grandson, Edward III (1327-77). Immediately we have a glorious and inventive mixture of pure heraldry and heraldically inspired decoration, some of the designs of which were to prove remarkably long lasting. But there were also to be many non-heraldic designs on the gold coinage – the equally long lasting 'angel' design, showing St Michael spearing a dragon, for instance – and the silver coinage remained entirely free of heraldry until the reign of Henry VII (1485-1509).

Top: English penny of Edward I; Scottish penny of Alexander III.
Above: Testoon of Henry VII.
Opposite: Noble of Edward III; gold seal of Henry VIII (1509-47).

The development of the Royal Arms

Since the thirteenth century the arms used by the monarchs of the British Isles have frequently been adapted to record the coming together of kingdoms. Before the two Acts of Union, which created the modern United Kingdom, it was not political but 'personal' union that heraldry recorded – the situation arising when one king ruled (or claimed to rule) two distinct kingdoms.

French arms 'ancient' *(opposite above)* **and 'modern'** *(opposite below)*

In 1340, Edward III's claim to the throne of France was represented heraldically by 'quartering' the French Royal Arms with those of England. In 1405, under Henry IV, the *fleurs-de-lys* (stylised lilies) in the French quarter were reduced to three, reflecting the equivalent adjustment made by Charles V of France. The claim to the French throne was to remain purely 'titular' – a ritual gesture maintained (like other monarchs' claims to the crown of Jerusalem) for centuries. It was only in 1801 that the claim was formally dropped, and the French lilies could finally be removed from the Royal Arms.

11

A similar burst of heraldic inventiveness and diversity was seen a century later on the coinage of James I (1603-25), who – as explained on page 13 – was the first monarch to incorporate the arms of Ireland into the unified picture. The seventeenth-century coinage, in fact, was highly heraldic in content, creating many durable conventions of design, alongside other non-heraldic imagery such as Britannia, who first appeared in 1672. Even the mid-century experiment with non-royal government, the parliamentary Commonwealth, produced heraldic coinage – it was, in fact, by far the most overwhelmingly heraldic of all English coinages, before or since.

The Restoration of the monarchy in 1660 saw a return to the pre-Commonwealth Royal Arms, and the establishment of another durable heraldic type, in which the arms of the four kingdoms (England, France, Ireland and Scotland) were represented on four separate shields. This interestingly 'analytical' approach, continued on the silver coinage without a break for a century, was joined under George II (1727-60) by a series of bold representations of the integral whole on the gold coinage. Here, as on the silver coinage and in many other contexts beyond coinage, the originally austere and medieval aesthetic of heraldry was gaily surrendered to the full floridity of the eighteenth- and early nineteenth-century engraver's art.

Above: Spur-ryal of James I.
Below: Broad of Oliver Cromwell.

Arms of Ireland

Tudor expansionism had no effect on the Royal Shield. In 1536 Henry VIII incorporated Wales into England; that year's Statute of Wales unequivocally enacts that 'The countrey or dominion of Wales shall... continue for ev(er) from henseforthe incorporated united and annexed to and with this his realme of Englande'. As a part of his English domain, it made no sense for Wales to have its own quarter in the arms. And even in 1541, when the same king raised the status of his Irish dominions from a subject lordship and started calling himself King of Ireland, his arms as King of England remained unaltered. He and his immediate successors did, however, use a separate shield with a design of a gold harp in a blue field *(left)* – a new design for a new (or, at any rate, resurrected) kingdom.

The Stuart Royal Arms

 When James VI of Scotland inherited the English throne in 1603, the new personal union of the crowns had to be matched by heraldic 'union of the Armes of both Realmes England and Scotland'. Much thought was given to how to achieve this; the version preferred by the King, seen here *(top)*, gave the harp design for Ireland its own quarter. That left three quarters to share between England and Scotland; problems of precedence were dealt with by having alternative versions for use in England and Scotland. With the addition of a small inner shield (an 'inescutcheon') showing the arms of Nassau following the accession of William and Mary in 1689, William being Prince of Orange and ruler of the Netherlands, the arms adopted by James I remained in use until 1707 *(left)*.

Post-Union Arms of Queen Anne

The Act of Union of 1707 incorporated England and Scotland as one kingdom, and Queen Anne (1702-14) became Queen of Great Britain, Ireland and (in a titular fashion) France. There was, perhaps, no need for a change in her coat of arms; but a new design was instituted, giving Scotland and England equal billing in the first and fourth quarters. This distinguished between the political union forming Great Britain, and the personal one which still bound Great Britain to Ireland (and, in theory, to France). The component parts of the new design were analysed separately on the coinage *(right)*.

Top: Crown of James I. *Left*: Five guineas of William and Mary. *Right*: Crown of Queen Anne.

Hanoverian Royal Arms (1714-1801)

 From the accession of George I in 1714, Britain and Ireland were bound in a purely personal union to Hanover. It was consistent with earlier practice for the Hanoverian Royal Arms to get a quarter of their own, ousting the second of the two quarters standing for Great Britain (*left*).

Hanoverian Royal Arms (1801-37)

 In 1801 a second Act of Union created the United Kingdom of Great Britain and Ireland, and prompted a radical rethink of heraldry and titulature which saw the end of the French *fleurs-de-lys*, along with the ancient, empty claim to the French throne. This meant that three of the four elements making up the Royal Arms stood for the constituent parts of a political union: England, Ireland and Scotland (*right*).

Left: Five guineas of George II. *Right*: Guinea of George III.

Current Royal Arms from 1837

 The odd one out was now the Hanoverian quarter; it was taken out from the scheme of quarters and placed in an inescutcheon beneath the ceremonial cap worn by George III (1760-1820) as Elector of Hanover – replaced by a crown in 1816 when Hanover became a kingdom (*left*).

The quarters for the home nations were redistributed to form the main shield; and when, in 1837, the crowns of the United Kingdom and of Hanover went their separate ways, the inescutcheon disappeared and the modern arrangement of the Royal Arms was at last arrived at (*right*).

Left: Half-crown of George III. *Right:* Sovereign of Victoria.

The die engraver had plenty of other material to engage with, of course. The seated Britannia remained a consistent presence, joined in 1816 by Benedetto Pistrucci's famous semi-naked St George, stabbing at the dragon with a short sword. On the smaller silver coins, the main reverse design was often a simple statement of value, within a wreath with the royal crown above. But while Britannia and St George have continued in classicising style down to our own day, ten years into the reign of Queen Victoria heraldry was dramatically returned to a 'medieval' idiom, with the so-called 'gothic crown' issue of 1847. Interestingly, this issue returned to the analytical approach of breaking down the Royal Arms onto four separate shields – an approach that was to last until 1935 with a brief reprise on the 1953 Coronation crown.

The durability of this design is fascinating when one considers that, after 1801, the combined Royal Arms no longer represented a personal union but a single political entity. It is a clear indication of the fact that, when it comes to heraldry, British coinage design has always felt free to look closely at individual parts of the whole, even at times when the reality and strength of the political union was beyond question. In fact, within the restricted, even cramped compass of a coin, the decision to focus on the separate parts of a design has often enhanced the other, simultaneously pursued, approach of looking at the whole thing together.

Even before the end of the nineteenth century heraldic design on the coinage worked free of the grip of extreme Victorian 'gothic', but it did retain a bold and clear style that owed more to the Middle Ages than to Georgian neo-classicism. Down to the end of the pre-decimal coinage, in fact, British coin designers represented the Royal Arms in a sturdy, confident fashion that did much for the heraldry, and interacted well with the various non-heraldic designs of the same period. The decimal definitive issues since 1971 have, largely, taken a rather different approach. Mostly heraldic in content, they returned to an almost neo-classical naturalism, most evident in the case of the lion on the ten pence piece. By focusing on the Royal Crest and selected royal badges, they steered clear of the shield and were able to treat Scotland, Wales and (after the introduction of the twenty pence piece in 1982) England separately.

Heralds and their artists have often had input into coin design over the centuries. Among the artists producing coin and medal designs for the Royal Mint there have always been some starting from a solidly heraldic training and background. But representation and re-interpretation of the Royal Arms, particularly on a definitive issue, are not just the preserve of heraldic experts. Often the most successful and novel heraldic work has been produced by those with a different starting point altogether. Matt Dent's new designs are a case in point. True to heraldry, they analyse without fragmenting and thereby achieve a goal aimed at by many of his predecessors – that of enhancing the unified whole.

....

Left: Unissued half-crown
of Edward VIII dated 1937.
Top right: Gothic crown
of Victoria, 1847.
Right: Decimal ten pence coin.

What does the 'unified whole' of British heraldry represent? Although the Royal Coat of Arms has told many stories over the centuries, what it now records is political union between kingdoms; by a circuitous route, though not in an unguided way, it has ended up as a form of pictorial shorthand for the two Acts of Union. Whether this is the best way to represent the modern United Kingdom is debated and indeed doubted by some. One frequent cause for comment is the absence of Wales, explained in historical terms at the foot of page 12; Wales did not, in short, enter the Union by the same door as Scotland and Ireland. It might be held that Henry VIII's decisions to incorporate Wales into England in 1536 but turn Ireland into a kingdom of its own five years later were arbitrary and an unsuitable basis for modern national symbolism – especially since he himself did not (as explained in the timeline) regard it as a basis for admitting Ireland to a combined coat of arms with his other realms.

The Welsh absence from the arms of the United Kingdom has, in fact, often been addressed at high level, with the Privy Council considering the question in 1910 and 1952, and – after much deliberation – eventually deciding to represent Wales heraldically in other ways than on the Royal Shield. This was a solution already tried: in 1800 the old Welsh badge of the red dragon on a grassy mount, used by Henry VII as a mark of his descent from Cadwaladr, was restored to status as a royal badge; today it is much better known (in slightly schematised form) as the flag of Wales, but it continues in its royal role today as a royal badge for Wales, and in

Below: Arms of the Prince of Wales. *Opposite top:* Arms of Owain Glyn Dŵr from a harness boss. *Opposite below:* A wyvern supporting a banner of the arms used by the medieval princes of Gwynedd, as remembered in an early Tudor manuscript.

the full Coat of Arms of the Prince of Wales, along with his other badge of three ostrich feathers. The Privy Council felt that to admit Wales to the Sovereign's shield would be tantamount to rewriting history, as well as courting the difficulty of what to do about other units within the Union that had been similarly annexed, or indeed those parts of the Commonwealth bound to the United Kingdom by the personal union of sharing the same monarch.

The logic of this response is not unassailable. Perhaps more insurmountable would be the practical difficulty of choosing a coat of arms to stand for Wales. By unfortunate coincidence, the very period when heraldry was developing among the indigenous rulers of Wales – the late thirteenth century – was the period in which English power was growing and pre-empting the unity that might have led to the creation of a truly national heraldic design. The red dragon has not itself been historically shown on a shield. Many have felt the best candidate to be the fine red and gold arms used by the princes of Gwynedd, who mounted considerable resistance to Edward I; similar arms were later used by Owain Glyn Dŵr, in the early fifteenth century. This design is already used in the middle of the arms of the Prince of Wales and certainly fits well with the existing Royal Arms in stylistic terms – but whether an antiquarian choice like this would satisfy modern Welsh requests for heraldic representation is another matter.

The two versions of the Royal Arms used in the United Kingdom: England, Wales and Northern Ireland (*above*) **and Scotland** (*right*)

The full Royal Coat of Arms is made up of not just a shield but supporters (the lion and unicorn, who support the shield), a crest (a crowned lion on top of the helmet, in different poses in the two versions), a motto (again, different in the two versions) and various adjunct badges and insignia such as those of the Orders of the Garter and the Thistle. The supporters and mottoes in particular have changed many times throughout the course of history.

Above and right: Great Seals of the United Kingdom.

Another question that might be raised is more general. Can the Royal Arms really function as a symbol of nationhood on the modern coinage, regardless of how well they record the constituent parts of the nation? The arms are, after all, personal to the Sovereign, and have never been 'released' for general use in the same way that the Union Flag is sometimes regarded.

It is true that the Royal Arms belong to the Crown, and are used by government and the executive as the Crown's representatives. In that sense the appearance of royal heraldry on the modern coinage can be seen as a direct continuation of the principle that coins are minted in the Sovereign's name and authority. But in fact – as the development discussed above indicates – the modern Royal Arms have come to represent the political make-up of the United Kingdom very closely, and to reflect none of the other personal aspects of the monarch, as would have been the case in the heraldry of many European monarchies. The Queen is Sovereign of the Isle of Man and of the separate Channel Islands, all of which have their own coats of arms; but these do not appear in the Royal Arms of the United Kingdom. Nor, for that matter, do the arms of the various Commonwealth countries of which she is Queen. This is an unusual British approach, quite distinct from that of most Continental monarchies throughout the ages. Indeed, it is different from the earlier British approach. Looking from a domestic perspective, then, the modern Royal Arms have clearly been fashioned to fulfil, as well as possible, the role of national symbol for the United Kingdom. That our national symbol should belong to the Queen is part and parcel of living in a monarchy, where government and civil service activity is carried on in her name and royal prerogative is largely exercised by elected politicians.

In that sense, for the coinage to display the Royal Arms is no odder than for the letters HM to appear before the names of naval vessels and prisons. It is in fact even more natural, because the association between coinage and royal heraldry is so old and so successful visually. It is also less irksome to those who dislike its implications, because no coinage issue is universal and all-encompassing. Even the fine new definitive issue will not oust existing coinage, but supplement it. Welsh heraldry will continue to circulate on millions of one pound pieces and other coins to be issued in the future. Non-heraldic reverses will remain in use and be added to by bold, non-traditional designs. But for the Royal Mint to give space to a fascinating, progressive and unusual exploration of one of the most timeless themes of British coinage is both a natural step and an exciting one.

Above: Reverses of circulating one pound coins showing symbols of Wales.

Christopher Ironside and the designs for the decimal coinage

Catherine Eagleton

For hundreds of years, the coinage of the United Kingdom had been based on the pound of 240 pence, or 20 shillings. There had been earlier discussions about the possibility of decimalising the currency, but these gained new impetus in the 1960s, and in 1961 a committee of inquiry was appointed, chaired by Lord Halsbury, to consider how the currency of the United Kingdom might be decimalised. This major event would have to involve redesigning the coinage, but it was also an opportunity to change the shapes, sizes, metals and denominations of the coins in use by millions of United Kingdom businesses and individuals. Even before the committee reported, the design process had begun, but was kept secret because the plans to decimalise had not yet been announced to the public. A number of artists were invited to submit designs to a closed competition. Christopher Ironside, one of these artists, was already an accomplished medal designer, so it was natural that he was invited to take part. His designs were eventually chosen for the new decimal coins, but the process of finalising them took six years. The archive of his drawings and plaster casts, in the collections of the British Museum, tracks this long process.

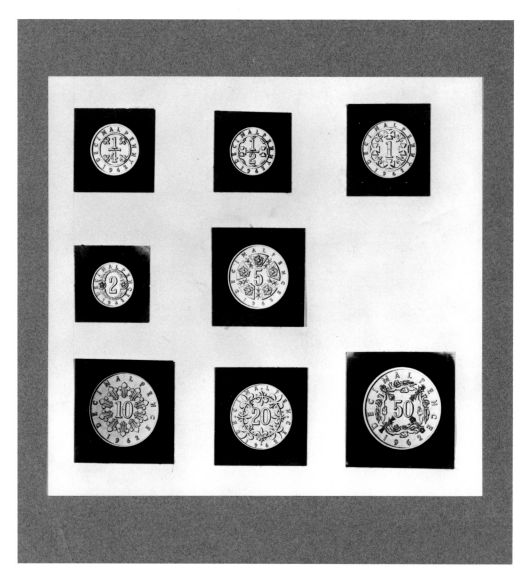

Above: This set of designs, dated 1962, is the earliest surviving in the Ironside archive.

Work still continued through 1963, and Ironside concentrated on several sets of designs. The denominations to be introduced were not yet finalised, but heraldic themes featured strongly. Each set of designs submitted was prepared as pencil drawings, which were then photographed and reduced in size, before being mounted on a single board for the Royal Mint Advisory Committee to consider.

Below: Some of the preparatory drawings for Set A.

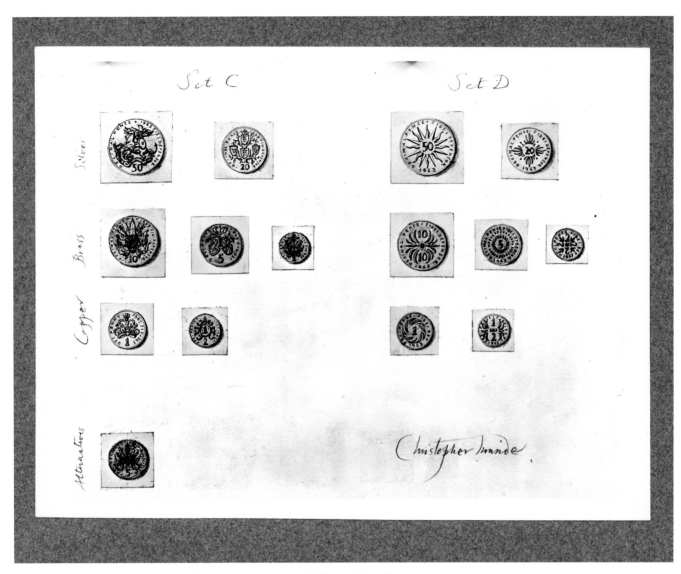

Above: Set C and Set D designs, showing very different ideas for the decimal coin designs.

Below: Drawings for one penny and two, five and ten pence coins in Set B.

Later in 1963, a final set of designs was agreed upon, and these were made into plaster models, for denominations from a farthing to twenty pence. Some of these were finished by the end of 1963; others, including the ten pence coin featuring St George and the dragon, and the two pence coin showing Britannia, were more difficult to get right.

The new farthing was to have a design based on an entwined rose and thistles, while the halfpenny was to have the Welsh dragon on its reverse. Christopher Ironside preferred to work on plaster in reverse *(above)*.

Work on the ten pence, showing St George and the dragon, continued into 1964. Fitting a complex figure onto the reverse, along with the inscription, numeral and year, posed a particular design challenge.

29

Another difficult design was the figure of Britannia for the two pence coin. One of the options considered in 1963, and rejected, was to overlap the numeral on the figure.

In December 1963, Christopher Ironside wrote to Jack James, Deputy
Master of the Royal Mint, that 'when I get a pencil in my hand to design
another Britannia I begin to feel foggy between the ears.' Nevertheless,
he prepared many different versions of Britannia in 1964 and 1965,
and a final design was at last approved by the Royal Mint Advisory
Committee completing the set.

Just as the designs were finished, however, there was a change of plan. In March 1966 Jack James asked to see Christopher Ironside, poured him a large gin and tonic, and told him that, although he had won the closed competition to design the new decimal coins, these designs would not be used. Instead, the Chancellor of the Exchequer, James Callaghan, was to announce a public competition to design the new coins. Ironside would have to start again, from scratch. Drawing on the experiences of the preceding four years, and using some of the same emblems and designs as in the first competition, he submitted four sets of designs to the public competition.

Ironside won the second competition and the designs were
revised and reworked. The now-familiar reverses, featuring Britannia,
the lion, thistle, Prince of Wales's feathers, portcullis and crown,
began to take shape.

Above: This early sketch from Christopher Ironside's notebook shows different possible versions of the Prince of Wales's feathers. Several of these were worked up into detailed drawings, before one was selected as the final design.

Opposite: The Prince of Wales's feathers design as it appeared on the new two pence coins.

A design for the fifty pence showing the Royal Arms made it all the way through to trial pieces before it was decided to adopt Britannia instead.

Above: The Queen and Prince Philip at the Royal Mint in December 1968 with Christopher Ironside (right) and Jack James, Deputy Master of the Royal Mint (centre left).

The introduction of the new coins, and the decimalisation of the United Kingdom currency, was an enormous task. In the lead up to D-Day, 15 February 1971, there were radio programmes to tell people about the new currency, and the Royal Mint and government had to consider worst-case scenarios including public rejection of the coins, or price inflation due to the rounding up of new prices. Thousands of millions of coins were struck in preparation, and cash registers and vending machines had to be adapted to the sizes, shapes and weights of the new coins. Some criticised the new designs for being old fashioned, but Christopher Ironside's response was that he 'wanted to be traditional as far as possible. I was not designing for myself, but for everyone else.' A year later, he elaborated his view of the role of a coin designer:

'The work of a great many artists who are geniuses is never recognised and probably eventually disappears. But if one is a coin designer, one's work lasts possibly long after death, everyone becomes familiar with it and it forms a small part of the history of the country for which it was designed, and one becomes famous. Not because one is a genius, or a saint, or a monster, but simply because one is a coin designer.'

Continuity through change: the Royal Mint Advisory Committee

Sir Christopher Frayling

I have chosen the title 'Continuity through change' for various reasons. First, because when we were discussing the edge inscription for a Golden Jubilee commemorative coin I approached my friend Andrew Motion – the Poet Laureate – to see if he had any thoughts. He suggested 'continuity through change', which seemed to me an appropriate sentiment as well as an excellent joke. Sadly, the inscription never made it to the actual coin, but it has nevertheless stuck in my mind. Second, because the phrase is an apt summary of the kinds of aesthetic choice we on the Advisory Committee have to make, when deciding on the design of new coins and medals. A well-known designer said to me recently 'everyone has three things in their pocket or bag: keys, mobile phones and coins. Keys have remained much the same for hundreds of years, mobile phones are redesigned every month, while coins are somewhere between the two – nearer keys than phones'. And third, I chose the phrase because it points to surprising continuities and consistencies between the work of the Committee today and the story of the British coinage since the early 1920s. So 'Continuity through change' it is.

The Royal Mint Advisory Committee – or, to give it its full name, the Royal Mint Advisory Committee on the Design of Coins, Medals, Seals and Decorations – began life in its current form in 1922, the brainchild of Colonel Robert Johnson, who had become Deputy Master of the Royal Mint earlier that year. There had in fact been an ad hoc Committee in 1891-92, to help select the new coinage designs of 1893 – with artistic and financial representatives on it – but that was dissolved when its job was done. The new Committee would be very different. Colonel Johnson came from a career in the Scottish Education Department, and Customs and Excise – which do not immediately strike one as ideal qualifications – but he proved to be a decisive, determined and canny individual. Johnson was highly critical of the coins which had recently been struck by the Royal Mint, and of the quality of First World War medals – medals which had been designed following competitions organised by the War Office, the Board of Trade (for the Merchant Navy) and the Admiralty. And he was keen to give responsibility for design back to the Royal Mint, to keep his skilled workforce intact and the Royal Mint's presses busy during the lull after the 1918 storm, and above all to raise 'numismatic art' to levels

it had enjoyed a century before – in the heyday of Benedetto Pistrucci's crown of George III (1818) with its celebrated classical reverse design of St George slaying the dragon, George mounted on a Parthenon-style horse; and the Victorian era of the Wyon family of engravers (Thomas, Thomas, William and Leonard) – with their Gothic Revival patterns and almost equally celebrated 'bun' penny of 1860, the portrait not 'cut' at the neck but with the shoulder-line reaching downwards to the coin's border. Pistrucci in particular had had the confidence to break with the long tradition of featuring an heraldic device of arms on the reverse: a brave thing to do, and in Johnson's view, a triumphant success. Maybe a committee of experts would help to bring back that kind of aesthetic confidence – as well as protecting a civil servant like himself from 'the autocratic tendencies of over-mighty bureaucrats'. This was a task, he felt, far too sensitive to be left to the Royal Mint officials acting alone.

Another advantage of 'concentrating all the work in one hand', he said, was the possibility of building up 'a School of artists who will find it worth their while to specialise in the production of coins and medals, and thereby return to the good old times'.

The immediate trigger for the Committee was the War Office's proposal to organise a competition – on behalf of the Army Council – for a General Service Medal to be awarded to those who had taken part in post-Armistice operations in Iraq and elsewhere in the Middle East. Asked by the Treasury for his opinion of the idea, Johnson replied that it was news to him that the Army Council had become an authority on design. Surely it was much better to give responsibility for the selection of the artist and the preparation and finishing of the design, to well-briefed professionals at the Royal Mint. Their Lordships at the Treasury agreed and so Johnson proposed an independent standing Committee 'with all the distinguished sculptors, numismatists and art critics that we can think of', a Committee that would advise the Deputy Master on artistic matters, keep him in touch with rising talent and generally encourage 'the art of producing medals, coins and decorations', with results that would be communicated, through the Deputy Master to the Master of the Royal Mint, the Chancellor of the Exchequer himself – by whom recommendations would be forwarded for royal approval. Those departments sponsoring medals – such as the War Office – could if they wished nominate a representative as an observer for that item on the agenda so they would at least be consulted. And they still do, by the way.

By the end of April 1922, it had been decided that the Committee ought to be appointed by the King, George V, and that its membership should always include a senior representative of the Sovereign. King George thought the idea 'perfectly right' and gave it his personal blessing. Unlike in 1891-92, the Committee would be a standing Committee.

The composition of the Committee, in the first instance, would be Johnson as Chairman; George Hill, Keeper of Coins and Medals at the British Museum; Sir Cecil Harcourt, Director of the Victoria & Albert Museum – apparently a 'vigorous-minded man' which sounded promising; the Earl of Crawford, First Commissioner of Works and a well-known art collector; Francis Derwent Wood – the short-fused Professor of Sculpture at the Royal College of Art; and Sir Frederick Ponsonby, Keeper of the Privy Purse, as the King's personal representative.

Johnson was at first not at all keen to have a sculptor on the Committee – because he was convinced that the decline in numismatic art was in large part the fault of sculptors who had no real understanding of the technologies of coin and medal work, and were no longer comfortable working in miniature. But in the end he was persuaded that to exclude sculptors would 'run the risk of trouble'. Even after one had been appointed the Royal Society of British Sculptors expressed its fears that a dictatorial Ministry of Taste had been formed. It was certainly a small Committee. If this really did represent all the relevant names 'we can think of', one can only conclude that Johnson's network did not extend much beyond clubland. There was only one practitioner, Derwent Wood, and he was there on sufferance. But Johnson was convinced that his Committee 'really know(s) the business and possess(es) highly critical faculties'. So, small but perfectly formed. It was gently pointed out at the time to Johnson that there were no actual designers of coins or medals on the list, which could be a problem, but he replied – with characteristic bluntness – that 'no distinguished medallist at present exists in this country'. So that was that. The membership would be expanded throughout the 1920s to include an expert on heraldry and a bit of extra fire-power in the sculpture department.

The first meeting – with two of the members absent in fact – took place in the Privy Purse Office at Buckingham Palace on 29 June 1922. From 1924 onwards, the more usual meeting place would be St James's Palace.

Looking through the Royal Mint Annual Reports of the 1920s and 1930s, there were various issues which kept recurring on the agenda: how to balance the rich heritage of British coinage – especially of 'the good old times' – with modernity and innovation; ditto for medals, such as those for the British Empire Exhibition of 1924, and ditto for the Great Seal of 1929; too much of the frozen hand of convention on the one hand and of modern for modern's sake on the other; how to find designers who fully understood the techniques of low-relief modelling as well as the processes of production, and who were prepared to take a close interest in them from start to finish; the relative advantages of the plastic and graphic arts; the practitioner's view and the historian's view; how to find designers of the calibre of, say, Percy Metcalfe – who produced the Irish Free State's successful new horse and fish and fowl designs, the so-called beast designs, getting round the usual abstract images of republicanism in an original way, coins with which the Committee had not of course been involved, though Johnson did write some very complimentary things about them; the Irish coins showed what could be done – but members often found it difficult to take such a bold aesthetic plunge; heraldry – at which George Kruger Gray was a *maestro* – or other national symbols; was there a place for heraldry in the contemporary world; which shields of arms should be used; how to prevent 'cliques' forming on the Committee; what kind of expertise should be represented around the table. In July 1931, Ponsonby of the Palace told Johnson that he thought the Committee was 'becoming more and more out of date, more and more out of touch with modern ideas, and more inclined to revert to the old ideas which have passed through the furnace and proved themselves to be sound'. And this was the view from *Buckingham Palace*. There was much talk in the air – which we know had reached the King – of design reform, of the Design and Industries Association, and of the relative lack of good young designers coming out of art schools – the subject of several government reports and official exhibitions in the early to mid-1930s. There was also the question of whether the royal family was seen to be in touch with the times. Maybe a modern artist on the Committee – such as the sculptor Charles Sargeant Jagger – would help its deliberations from being over-cautious and over-academic. Johnson did not altogether agree – he felt, as did most members of the Committee, that it had been quite modern enough, thank you very much – but Jagger was indeed appointed in January 1932. He died suddenly in November 1934.

Opposite: Designs for crown pieces by George Kruger Gray *(above)* and Percy Metcalfe *(below)*.

Although Derwent Wood was no longer a member (he had died in 1926, to be replaced by the Arts and Crafts disciple Robert Anning Bell), this issue of modernity versus tradition had recently been very much in the public eye, at Hyde Park Corner no less, in two high-profile commissions from Derwent Wood and Jagger: the Monument to the Machine Gunners and the Monument to the Royal Artillery. One, the Machine Gunners, was the last triumphalist gasp of Victorian 'new sculpture'. The other showed, with searing monumental realism, what the artillery in the First World War actually did. Jagger had been a student at the Royal College of Art, Derwent Wood had been a tutor, then Professor from 1918 onwards. So whenever I drive around Hyde Park Corner, I think of the apprentice outgrowing the sorcerer – the new generation taking over from the old, and the generosity of spirit this should ideally involve. But not too new. Henry Moore had also been one of Derwent Wood's students in fact, in 1921-23, and the Professor had written in his first year report on young H. Moore that 'Design not to my liking. Is much interested in carvings'; and in his third year report 'his design might show improvement – he appears somewhat limited in his interest of tradition in sculpture'. Equally,

Right: Monument to the Machine Gunners by Francis Derwent Wood.
Opposite: Monument to the Royal Artillery by Charles Sargeant Jagger.

ERECTED TO COMMEMORATE THE GLORIOUS HEROES OF THE MACHINE GUN CORPS

Charles Sargeant Jagger – the new up-and-coming generation – was on record as saying in December 1930 about one of Moore's 'Reclining Women': 'the sort of people who do it merely seek an early road to notoriety... like every other epidemic it will die a natural death'. Following Jagger's death, he was replaced on the Committee in 1934 by Percy Jowett, Head of the Central School and shortly – in April 1935 – to be appointed Principal of the RCA. He was scarcely a radical either: a gentle post-Impressionist painter about whom William Rothenstein wrote approvingly 'under his able guidance the College was unlikely to be industrialised'. No danger of industrial design, then.

But these changes of membership did lead to a slightly more contemporary approach to design – albeit one which was highly tentative at first. There was, for example, the 1934 King's Medal for Poetry, with entries from John Skeaping and Percy Metcalfe and a winning design by the illustrator Edmund Dulac. But then there was the strange case of the new Edward VIII coinage of 1936 – which involved with the King's agreement another expansion of the Committee, to include among its now 14 members Kenneth Clark

who joined in April 1936. Clark was to serve on the Committee from 1936 to 1945 and then from 1952 to 1975. He resigned in 1945 when he left the National Gallery, because 'I shall have no official position in the art world': but in his resignation letter he called the Committee 'one of the least onerous and most interesting' in his portfolio, and he was back seven years later.

The strange case involved at one time or another serious discussions at the Palace about whether the King should face to the left or to the right on his uncrowned effigy: numismatic tradition has succeeding monarchs facing alternate ways, and after George V it was the turn of the right-hand side; but the King much preferred the left-hand side for the uncrowned portrait, probably because it showed off to good advantage the parting in his hair – he had no problem about the right-hand side for the crowned portrait, where the crown covered up the parting; then there was the wax model of a coin mislaid somewhere in the lower depths of Buckingham Palace; and there was the unseemly squabble on the Committee itself – about the obverses – between the Humphrey Paget faction and the William McMillan RA faction. Humphrey Paget was one of the Royal Mint's panel of artists,

Portraits of Edward VIII by William McMillan *(above)* and Humphrey Paget *(opposite)*.

while the sculptor William McMillan was supported by the Royal Academy members, which was indeed becoming a faction. And this led to irretrievable breakdown – so the choice was left up to the King, who opted for Paget's obverse. In the event, of course, because of the abdication in December, no United Kingdom coins with or without portraits were ever issued. But it had been a close and ill-tempered thing. And Johnson, shortly before he died in 1938, with memories of 1936 still fresh, made comments about his 'rather turbulent' Committee. But the Committee had, he added, caused a steady and highly satisfactory improvement in the design of medals and to a lesser extent coins. Its expertise had, as he put it, sometimes saved him from error and infelicity. The correct shape of a Greek helmet could safely be left to the British Museum contingent, while Oswald Barron, the representative from the College of Arms, knew all about the finer points of heraldic accuracy. Which was very helpful. All in all, as Graham Dyer, former Secretary to the Committee, has justly concluded, 'to those of you who would complain of the designs which it recommend[ed], I would say that you should see all the others'.

It is instructive to look, for comparison, at what happened in the Irish Free State in roughly the same period – and specifically to look at the work of the Committee which selected the new coinage there in 1926-28, chaired by Senator W.B. Yeats. This was said at the time to be the first modern state to design an entire coinage all at once; having rejected decimalisation, they decided to retain the British denominations then in circulation. The design committee reported to the Minister of Finance, and it first met on 17 June 1926 – four years after the initial meeting of its British counterpart, on which it was based. Yeats wrote to his friend Edmund Dulac – who had recently created a very fine medal – outlining the process. There would be a limited competition for selected artists, a proportion of whom would be Irish. The Committee would select in advance the symbols or emblems to be put on the coins, following advice from the Royal Irish Academy, the Royal Society of Irish Antiquaries, the Royal Hibernian Society and from members of the public, in response to a newspaper notice. But they would leave the visual treatment to the artist. The submissions as presented would be anonymous.

Yeats wrote to Dulac:

> 'Every coin will have a harp on one side but we can put what we like on the other. I am pressing on the Committee certain simple symbols which we can all understand as expressions of national products – say a horse, a bull, a barley sheaf, a salmon, a fox or hare, and a greyhound. Somebody else urges symbols of industries but we have so few industries and doubt the decorative value of a porter bottle. The Government will have to pass our symbols, or prefer others. We will probably only insist on their being very simple – emblems or symbols, not pictures.'

The idea that the whole range of coins should 'tell one story' originally came to Yeats from the artist William Orpen, while Dr Oliver St John Gogarty proposed to him a horse's head – to match a Sicilian coin in his collection.

In the event, the design Committee – which had a similar *ex officio* membership to its British counterpart: the President of the Royal Hibernian Academy; the Director and former Director of the National Gallery of Ireland; a silversmith; and a Secretary from the Department of Finance – went with the animal products rather than products in general, dropped the barley sheaf, the fox and the greyhound, and added a hen and chicks, a pig, a woodcock and an Irish wolfhound instead: 'what better symbols could we find', wrote Yeats 'for this horse-riding, salmon-fishing, cattle-raising country?'.

The more noble or dignified creatures would be assigned to the higher denominations – the more humble types to the lower. One member of the Committee preferred a greyhound or harrier to a wolfhound because 'on the only occasion known to him when hare and wolfhound met, the wolfhound ran away'. But the wolfhound remained. Later, the Minister diplomatically suggested adding a ram to the list of symbols as a possible alternative to the pig – because of 'the ridicule with which [the pig] is associated in connection with this country'. The hen and chicks were thought by some to be too homely, but the Committee replied that they regarded this as an advantage 'since it will make an immediate appeal to farmers – and especially to their wives and daughters to whom the care of poultry is a particular concern'. Photographs of Greek and Carthaginian coins (of between 430 and 342 BC) – featuring horses, a bull and a hare – were circulated to the seven selected artists, three of them Irish or Irish-American – together with reference materials on Gaelic script and pictures of the Trinity College and Dalway harps. The other selected artists were British, Serbian, Swedish and Italian. Edmund Dulac was not among the chosen few.

Opposite: Irish Free State coins by Percy Metcalfe.
Below: Poetry Medal by Edmund Dulac.

It was perhaps as well that the submissions were presented anonymously, because the Committee's unanimous choice on 15 February 1927 turned out to be a Yorkshire-born Englishman, an ex-RCA student (who had studied under Edward Lantéri and Derwent Wood) and Charles Sargeant Jagger's studio assistant who had been recommended to the Committee by the British School in Rome – Percy Metcalfe no less, who had recently designed the Great Seal and assorted British Empire Exhibition medals. Although the Committee voted denomination by denomination, Metcalfe won them all. The Irish nationalist Maud Gonne, on hearing the news, thundered back to Yeats that the Committee had chosen a coinage 'designed by an Englishman, minted in England, representative of English values, and paid for by the Irish people'.

The whole process, following the selection of Metcalfe, took from February 1927 to April 1928 and seven extra meetings – in October 1927 the Committee got to the point of threatening to resign *en masse* unless the to-ing and fro-ing stopped. But, whatever his reservations, Yeats in the end was very pleased with the final recommendation, as was his Committee. The British press was particularly positive about the outcome: 'the most beautiful coinage in the modern world', wrote the *Manchester Guardian*, to which the *Evening Standard* added 'we may well be jealous of the beautiful new Irish coins'. They have since become accepted as modern classics, the nearest approximation of classical Greek coins to be produced in the twentieth century.

½d

Returning to the Royal Mint Advisory Committee, and moving on to its deliberations of more recent times, I was approached in November 2000, to sound out whether I would be prepared to take on the chairmanship of the Committee – in succession to His Royal Highness Prince Philip, no less, who had occupied the specially-created post of President of the Committee since March 1952, 48 years before – with the Deputy Master as nominal Chairman. One of Prince Philip's first tasks had been to help select designers for the coins and medals of the new reign. Then there had been the steering of the Committee through the great decimalisation recoinage of the late 1960s. Not to mention four separate effigies of Her Majesty The Queen from 1952 onwards – skilfully reconciling Prince Philip's roles of Consort and Chairman. His Presidency had given the Committee great status, as well as giving unprecedented weight to its design decisions. A very hard act to follow. Nevertheless, I accepted with alacrity and chaired my first meeting in February 2001. It should be noted at this point

that the Committee no longer meets in St James's Palace – but usually at Cutlers' Hall in the City, and sometimes at Goldsmiths' Hall, Skinners' Hall, or the Cabinet Office, the Treasury, or – thanks to the Lord Chamberlain, currently the Earl Peel – in Buckingham Palace. Entering the Palace by the Privy Purse Door – on the right-hand side of the façade – we have met a couple of times in the Chinese Dining Room, a flamboyant example of early nineteenth-century red and gold Chinoiserie, which Queen Victoria admired so much when she saw it at the Royal Pavilion in Brighton that she ordered the room to be moved wholesale to Buckingham Palace – 'the mantelpiece', as Marina Warner (Committee member 1986-1993) has put it, 'astir with a thousand dragons spitting at you'. It is a wonderful, if slightly odd, setting for discussions of modernity and tradition – with the spitting dragon, the long mahogany table, the tall windows facing the Mall – especially when the Guards' Band is playing the Monty Python theme tune in the courtyard below, as happened once.

Coinage portraits of the Queen by Mary Gillick, Arnold Machin, Raphael Maklouf and Ian Rank-Broadley.

By far the most important, and interesting, Committee discussions on my watch, have been about the competition to redesign the six denominations of United Kingdom circulating coins from the penny to the fifty pence: the new definitive reverses. With the exception of the 'Tudor rose' twenty pence piece, which was introduced in 1982, the reverses of the coins from the 'portcullis' penny to the 'ostrich/Prince of Wales's feathers' two pence to the 'thistle' five pence to the 'lion' ten pence to the 'Britannia' fifty pence (unveiled in 1969, a year after the others) were all designed by Christopher Ironside in the lead-up to decimalisation, following a public competition – at the suggestion of James Callaghan: 83 entrants with 900 designs, in the end. All with the words NEW PENCE incorporated into the design. As the then Deputy Master Jack James put it, although the winning designs were 'new in style [they] have for the most part a long numismatic history', with a strong sense of tradition, of the emblems of Britain. They were elegant and they were clear, uncluttered – important at the time of such a complicated change. They were also traditional. Christopher Ironside taught life drawing part-time at the RCA in the 1960s, and had been recommended jointly by the Royal Designers for Industry and the Royal College of Art.

Well, in 2005 it was felt that the time had now come to introduce a new series of designs, the first since decimalisation – and so a competition was publicly announced in August 2005 with the words 'The Royal Mint invites members of the public to make their mark on history'. This competition would, we agreed, be open to the public – and individual invitations would simultaneously be sent to a selection of 18 professional artists and designers who were either experienced in coin design or who might respond in a particularly imaginative way. Also, to seven members of the Royal Mint Engraving Team, to three heraldic artists, and to overseas designers who had designed the coinages of Hungary, Iceland and the Czech Republic. So we would be judging designs from the interested public as well as the professionals. Unlike the Irish coinage of the 1920s, we would not be prescribing themes in advance. And, if the new ideas did not match up to Christopher Ironside's, then we reserved the right not to make any change at all.

Right: Drawing for the reverse of the twenty pence piece by William Gardner, 1982. *Opposite:* Posters published by the Decimal Currency Board.

DECIMAL CURRENCY BOARD

15th February 1971

On D Day the £ stays the same

...but the same £ will be made up of 100 new pence

DECIMAL CURRENCY BOARD

15th February 1971

On D Day there will be 100 new pence in the £

...so each <u>new</u> penny will be worth more than two <u>old</u> pennies

---

DECIMAL CURRENCY BOARD

When you go decimal shopping, remember

10/- = 50p
2/- = 10p
1/- = 5p

So sixpence equals 2½p

DECIMAL CURRENCY BOARD

Only these three 'coppers' will be new on D Day

½ new penny

1 new penny

2 new pence

all other coins stay the same

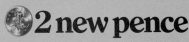

There seems to be no fixed time for how long definitive designs should remain unchanged. A process of redesigning the coinage tends to be started at the beginning of a new reign, and the twentieth century provided the Royal Mint with plenty of opportunities of this kind, including of course 1936. In particularly long reigns – such as those of George III or Queen Victoria – changes to the coinage happened for a number of reasons, but more often than not they represented a simple wish to refresh or renew the appearance of the coinage. After the 40 years since decimalisation, this was felt to be one of those times. It is an unusually long period of time for a series of coins to remain unchanged – you would need to go back as far as 1887 to find a series of reverses that has lasted as long.

By the closing date of 14 November 2005, a total of 526 people had submitted just over 4000 designs – the largest-ever response to a public competition of this type in Britain. There had been 15,148 hits on the competition website, and 915 information packs had been sent out. We decided early on that the initial sift should be done by a sub-committee of three members of the Committee under my chairmanship.

Heraldrycrests and Queen's Beastsroyalregaliachess
palacescastlespublicsculptureschalkfigureshist
BridgeBigBenbuildingssuchastheGlobeTheatre
umbrellacricketanchorpintofbeer**Nature**stones
seashellshengesandcliffsflowerswheatandcorn
Stubbs'horsesbulldogroyalcorgisLochNessm
Fairytalesincludingtheheraldicwhiterabbitfrom
Scienceatomtouniversegeometrygreatdiscoveri
telephoneboxradiomastLondonEyePostOfficeTow
differentcranes**Inventions**lightbulbjetenginecom
angles**Arts**ElgarShakespeareChaucerLewisCar
lightningandwindpowersourcesofpowerge
DesignSpitfirePennyFarthingConcordeMiniBeel
theclaspedhandsoffriendship**Sport**sportingachi
ofDavidetc**TheShippingNews**

This assembled on 18 November, and in a marathon meeting looked at all 4000 drawings. From 4000 drawings to 52 series, roughly half heraldic, half not: 52 series, 418 designs. Back to the main Committee on 8 December – also reporting on the rejected ones – which in further meetings winnowed the 52 series to 22 to 18 to 10 series, to 18 designs in three series. By July 2006, at Buckingham Palace, we had 18 designs, and each member of the Committee had been asked to select from among them, which took us down to two series with aspects of a third still being considered. This took us to the plaster-model stage. It was a fascinating process because what we were dealing with was nothing less than how Britain might be symbolised on the coinage in the early twenty-first century, at a time when discussions of 'Britishness' were and are very much in the news. Britishness, identity, inclusivity, citizenship, citizenship tests, heritage and contemporary – all were under discussion. How we see ourselves, and how much it matters. As it turned out, the entries approached the question – as you would expect – from many different angles. Here are my notes for the meeting of 8 December:

etscrestdeconstructed**Heritage**historichousesroyal
iclandscapes10DowningStreetAbbeyRoadTower
dfamousskylines**SocialLife**cupofteafishandchips
fBritainthelifecycleofanoaktreefromacorntooak
sectsfishbirdsanimalsfarmanddomesticecology
nsterpuffinsandharescommemorativepoppy
ceinWonderlandfolkloreCelticand'thegreenman'
includingGreenwichMeanTime**Designs**postbox
GherkinJodrellBanktelescopeelectricalequipment
uterandweb**Maps**ofthehomenationsfromvarious
llsymbolsofthearts**Weather**windcloudrainsun
ationincludingsolarwindandwater**Industrial**
veRadio**Values**equalitytolerancejusticedemocracy
ementsOlympics**Faith**symbolscrosscrescentStar

August2005TheRoyalM:
publictomaketheirmark
competitionwebsite915i
14Novemberdeadline52
drawingsinitiallonglisto:
MintAdvisoryCommitt:
2005SubCommittee8De
series26January2006/16M
31May2006shortlist10se
3series18designs5Octob
2series14March2007final
winner:DesignerZ

ntinvitesmembersofthe
onhistory15148hitsonthe
nformationpackssentout
6peoplesubmitted4003
52series418designsRoyal
emeetings18November
cember2005shortlist22
arch2006shortlist18series
ries13July2006shortlist
er2006/5December2006
ecisionmadecompetition

NotesonDesignerZTheRoyalShieldofArmsspread
acontemporarydesignidiomLikedthesimplicity
reachedthecoinagehavingbeenastrongthemewi
Althoughclearlysymbolicofunitythiswouldbemo
thefamilytogetherAtrulymodernseriesatlastButalso
portionsofthedesignRootedinitsowntimeItbreakstl
interestingcoinsandheraldryexplainingandexplori
beveryeffective

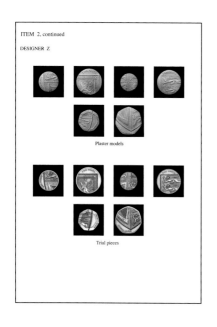

ITEM 2, continued

DESIGNER Z

Plaster models

Trial pieces

Above and opposite: Examples of
the presentation sheets showing
short-listed designs prepared
for the Royal Mint Advisory
Committee.

And, from a primary schoolboy, a selection of guns for the different
denominations: revolver, machine gun, automatic rifle and so on.
Very disturbing indeed.

These submissions raised many issues, which we discussed: should
the coins be a 'family' or not? They were not in 1968 – but should they
be now? Or should we select individual designs from various series,
on a pick and mix basis, or would this seem too much like 'design by
committee'? What should the balance be between traditional symbols
of the nation and modern ones? Heraldic, semi-heraldic or symbolic
or just illustrative? A traditional theme in a contemporary treatment,
or vice versa? And what of the specific symbols or icons themselves,
spread across the six coins? They had to have *gravitas* – but they had to
chime with today's society as well. How to communicate the historical
condition of the United Kingdom today? Can the iconographic
language of heraldry (with its unicorns and dragons) fit today's reality?
Or do we need some other image store? And they had to be technically
feasible too. Not just pictures but symbols. By the end of the July 2006
meeting – at the sign of the spitting dragon – two series of designs
had emerged as the clear front runners: very different series in very
different design styles by Designer E and Designer Z, and we were also
considering a third series, on a pick and mix basis. By 14 March 2007,
the Committee was ready to make its final recommendations, which
we had decided would involve not only the penny to the fifty pence
but the one pound coin as well, as a lynchpin of a whole series; as the
unifying coin. This idea emerged towards the end of the competition
process, bringing the total number of denominations to seven.

The discussion had stimulated some classic contributions from
Committee members – brilliantly transcribed by Kevin Clancy as our
Secretary who has ably succeeded Graham Dyer. Some of the heraldry
was 'too Hogwarts' or 'Narnia-like'. One set was deemed 'too gothic
and overbearing', like the parapet of a castle in a horror movie. If we
selected the eagle from one series and the white rabbit from another,
was there perhaps a danger that the one – the rabbit – 'might fall victim
to the predations of the other, the eagle'. One of the poppies reminded
the Committee of 'at best a rose and at worst a propeller'. Several series
were discarded as being like 'cheap, slot-machine money'.

Designer Z's idea – of spreading the Shield of the Royal Arms over all denominations – eventually emerged as the distinct front runner. The Committee liked very much the presentation of heraldry in a contemporary design idiom, the simplicity, and the strong 'family' idea. As was said at the time, 'this is a truly modern series at last', and 'deconstruction has at last reached coinage, having been a strong theme in fine art for some years'. The series was something like 'medieval coins struck to display portions of a design'. But it was also 'rooted in its own time' and 'it breaks the mould in an exciting way'. Maybe Designer Z's approach would stimulate public interest in coins and heraldry – explaining and exploring the different elements – which would certainly be a bonus. At a technical level, the matt/shiny contrast could well prove very effective. Although the series was clearly symbolic of national unity, this would be even more evident if the pound was added as a lynchpin bringing the 'family' together. The Committee was aware that such a relatively bold idea could prove controversial, and that there were some who would be uncomfortable with it, or indeed with any change. The decimalisation designs had, despite their excellence, not escaped criticism either. This was well-nigh inevitable.

Designer Z turned out to be the young graphic designer Matt Dent, who trained at Coleg Menai in Wales and at the University of Brighton – and who later said:

> '...a united design – united in terms of theme, execution and coverage over the surface of the coins...How to share four nations over six coins? Then I decided to look at heraldry. Perhaps the six coins could make up a shield by arranging the coins both horizontally and vertically. This piecing together of the elements of the Royal Arms to form one design had a satisfying symbolism – that of unity, four countries of Britain under a single monarch'.

So, in the year of the 10th anniversary of the Euro, the new coins have been launched. The curtain was raised on 2 April 2008 at the Tower of London – and I told John Humphrys on BBC Radio 4's *Today* programme that morning if all went wrong, it was only a short walk to Traitors' Gate...

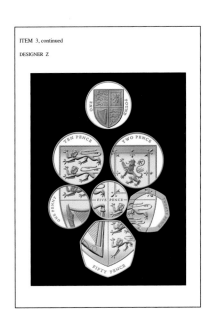

ITEM 3, continued

DESIGNER Z

In my time as Chairman of the Committee so far, I am particularly proud
of a number of coin designs.

The crown to celebrate the 100th anniversary of the *Entente Cordiale*
between Britain and France was designed by David Gentleman.
The brief suggested that as well as the usual State symbols such as flags
and crests and maps, the artists might be inspired by the symbolic female
figures of La Semeuse and Britannia – the sexy La Semeuse and the rather
more bossy Britannia. David combined the two in a sculptural treatment
that gave equal weight to both countries. This went down so well across
the Channel that the French Mint used it on their celebratory coins!
Quite an accolade.

A personal favourite of mine is the fifty pence piece marking the 250th
anniversary of the publication in 1755 of Dr Samuel Johnson's Dictionary
of the English Language. Artists approached the brief in many different
ways – books, learning, the glories of the English language, portraits of
Johnson himself, symbols of writing – but the design by the painter
Tom Phillips, his second United Kingdom coin design (his first was
the 2003 Coronation Anniversary crown with 'God Save the Queen' in
the middle of it), was the most convincing to the Committee. The word
'Fifty' and the word 'Pence', plural of penny – each with abridged
definitions, in eighteenth-century typefaces. They seemed to fit the
shape of the fifty pence so well. A terrific mixture of the traditional
and the modern, continuity and change.

Then there was the two-pound coin for the 300th anniversary of the
Act of Union between England and Scotland – ratified in the first half
of 1707 'that the two Kingdoms of England and Scotland shall...for
ever after be United into one Kingdom by the name of Great Britain'.
Yvonne Holton's design has the rose for England, the thistle for
Scotland, and two portcullises, quartered as if they were pieces
of a jigsaw – an original and memorable symbol of the Union.

Without I hope seeming to be too high-minded, I would like to conclude with three quotations about the Committee and the kind of work it does.

First, Colonel Johnson himself writing about the Irish coinage of the late 1920s – in words that could in my view equally well apply to our new definitive reverses. The parallels between the Irish example and our more recent deliberations are instructive:

> 'It embodies all the essential elements in the preparation of a worthy coinage…reliance upon an expert Committee without undue disturbance at the hands of Statesmen – a broad and liberal catholicity in the selection of the artist without regard to nationality or origin, ample time and an insistence upon the responsibility of the selected artist for satisfying himself that the dies represent the real intentions of his model, points which seem obvious enough when set out in cold print, but which in practice are so frequently disregarded with the most disastrous results.'

Second, Robin Porteous (numismatic adviser to the Committee), at a reception to mark the departure of Prince Philip from its Presidency:

> 'For many years we have sat round a table discussing banners and dragons and emblems of that kind and I suppose now feel a little like Sir Bedevere reminiscing by the lakeside – alas, without an Excalibur.'

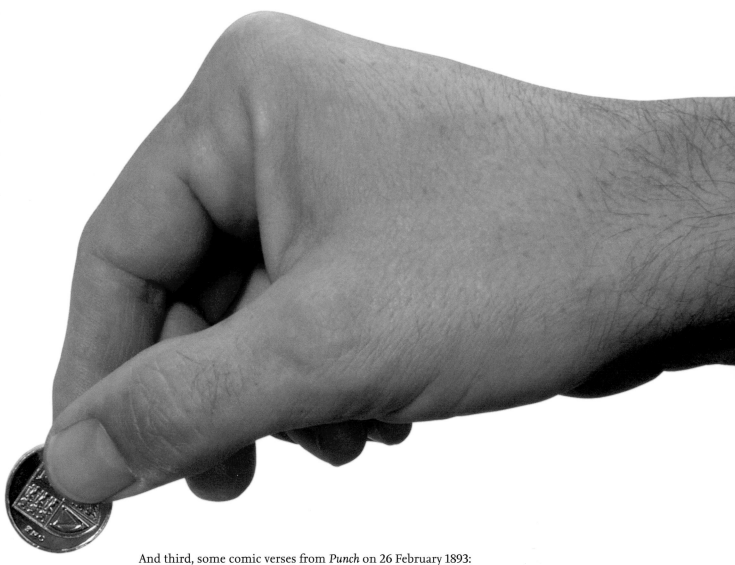

And third, some comic verses from *Punch* on 26 February 1893:
– about another Committee and another redesign of the coinage:

'Art will now adorn our purses
    Hitherto an artless place;
More than pictures, songs or verses,
    This should elevate the race.

Will the cabman now be willing,
    After driving half a mile,
To accept a high-art shilling,
    Not with oaths, but with a smile?

Will the porter at the station
    While his thanks pause on his lip,
Gaze in silent admiration
    At the beauty of his tip?

'Music hath', so Congreve stated,
    'Charms to soothe the savage breast';
Numismatic art is fated
    Maybe to be likewise blest.'

Making an impression

Matt Dent

My friend Daniel (aged eight) brought out a tissue from his pocket. He unwrapped it carefully, triumphantly, to show me the new five pence coin. It was the first one I had seen. And I remember thinking it looked very special and very tiny. There was something about its shininess which seemed to add to its smallness. It seemed so small, in fact, that it felt unusable compared to the old-size one. It is not that the coin had any financial significance for me – I mean, at eight years old what did I need to buy? I appreciated it on the merits of a beautiful object. Its gleam, size and rarity gave it such a worth, in my eyes, surpassing its five pence value, that I would have swapped a pound for it had I had one.

You always notice newly minted coins because they reflect up at you from the rest of the change in your hand. My parents would sometimes put aside a couple of shiny coins for me and my brother Dafydd. Their newness always demanded special care; being wrapped up in tissue paper and squirrelled away. Every so often I would come across an unusual coin; like a pound coin which had the same shape, same size, same colour as a normal one, and even had the same portrait of the Queen on one side, but this one's reverse depicted a prototype mobile phone with the text 'Isle of Man'. How unusual, I thought, and thus it merited squirrelling away in tissue paper.

We had a project during my Art Foundation course in Bangor, North Wales where we were asked to bring in an everyday object and justify its design. I think I took in a spoon, but I remember Owein Prendergast, my tutor, fishing out a coin from his pocket and talking about the remarkable amount of detail within the Queen's portrait over such little relief from the surface of the coin. 'You're not even talking millimetres, you're talking nanometres' he pointed out. I would not have thought it possible to sculpt a decent image of anything from such little relief, let alone a realistic portrait. But there it was; gems within the crown, the subtlest differentiation between the Queen's neck and jaw, there were wrinkles on her brow and even an earring. It was ridiculously good. It was not only a life-like portrait – I would be able to recognise Her Majesty should she sit next to me on the bus – but a work of art and a wonder of design. I do not think Owein's choice was challenged by anyone.

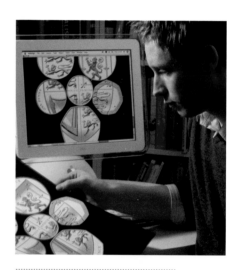

Above and opposite: Matt Dent preparing his designs and at the Tower of London after the unveiling of his new designs for the coinage.

Each of us has different associations with coinage. Much as I remember when and what I was doing around the time I saw my first new five pence coin, others may recall what they were up to upon seeing their first decimal coin, or two-pound coin, or updated portrait of the Queen. Looking at coins can be like flicking through a photo album – placing us at different moments in our lives.

The timing of the Royal Mint's new reverses competition was fortuitous as it happened to coincide with the conclusion of a year I spent working in New Zealand. I was now looking for a job back home which left me with time on my hands.

Alex, a friend of mine, emailed me a link to a page on *The Guardian* website which reported on the announcement of the competition. Moreover, it reported that the winning designs would be used as the new reverses for the circulating coinage. A competition like that does not happen often, and for someone like me with an interest in visual language it appealed enormously. I had to have a go.

For my *Design Trends* university project I gave 20 council planners, 20 builders, 20 graphic designers and 20 illustrators six different shapes of six different colours, and a blank canvas to arrange them as they wished. I documented the results to find out whether there were tendencies among the professions to arrange the shapes or colours in certain ways. The study resulted in a print and animation piece.

The brief which I downloaded from the Royal Mint's website suggested that the design should represent the constituent parts of the United Kingdom. Ok, fair enough I thought, but they are asking for designs for six coins so how is that going to work? Six coins do not divide particularly well between four countries. If I try to represent the countries how do I avoid a bias?

The competition seemed like an opportunity to tackle the set of six coins holistically. It appeared to me as an invitation for a united solution – united in terms of theme, content and style of execution.

I had an idea ticking away about a single design spread over several coins; each coin could show a part of a large image, which is constructed by arranging the individual coins in a certain way. This was an exciting idea – I had not seen an approach like this used on coinage before, and it was doubly exciting as I could imagine how people might enjoy playing with the coins and building the design up themselves. I could imagine children enjoying the puzzle as much as adults might.

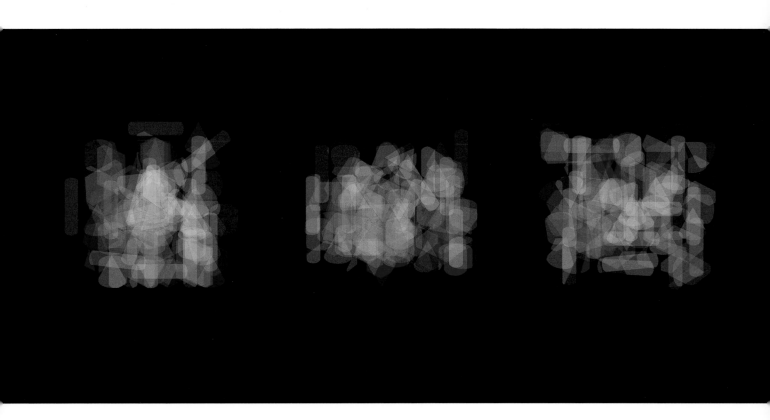

Since heraldry has been the basis of coinage design in Britain for hundreds of years, I wanted to try to tackle an heraldic approach. As a test to see whether the idea would work in an heraldic context, I printed an image of the shield of the Royal Arms, an emblem representative of the United Kingdom and therefore fitting the brief. Over this I placed the six coins (one penny to fifty pence), shifting them around, playing with the arrangement, before drawing around them and trimming them out to leave six discs each featuring a segment of the shield. The sections of shield on the individual discs appeared as abstract shapes – I saw curves, parallel lines, and ragged edges first and foremost before realising that these were the edge of a shield, strings of a harp and the shaggy mane of a lion. I saw six separate discs before realising that each belonged to a bigger picture.

On one level it was a puzzle, a game; 'I've got a corner piece here', 'this one continues the shield so it must go there…' as the separate pieces of a jigsaw were united. On another level there were deeper connotations; assembling the shield would illustrate how the separate elements of the Royal Arms come together and how the different countries comprise the United Kingdom. The solution appealed to me equally as a powerful message and as something I myself would want to play with.

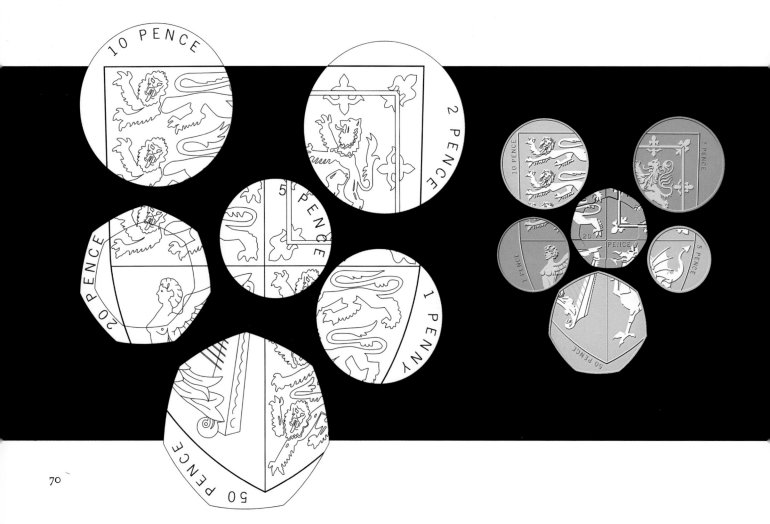

I was over the moon – my initial solution had got past the first stage. Over the course of the following months I was approached at regular intervals by Kevin Clancy (Secretary to the Royal Mint Advisory Committee) with the feedback coming from the most recent meeting of the Committee. Thankfully, the feedback was generally positive – along the lines of being asked to consider reviewing particular aspects of the design. This two-way communication channelled through Kevin continued throughout the development and into the production process.

It got to a point where the designs had been sufficiently adjusted and refined for the Committee to focus on how they worked in three dimensions; in this instance large-scale plaster models.

As a trained modeller, John Bergdahl had the expertise to realise my designs in this way. Through his skill he brought my designs to life – adding details like muscle mass, wisps of hair and fur – fixing the design in large-scale three-dimensional plaster models. I could now tilt the models and see how they responded to the light, I could run a finger over the textures and feel the lion's mane – enjoying for real those aspects that I could only imagine up until that point. The designs looked and felt brilliant.

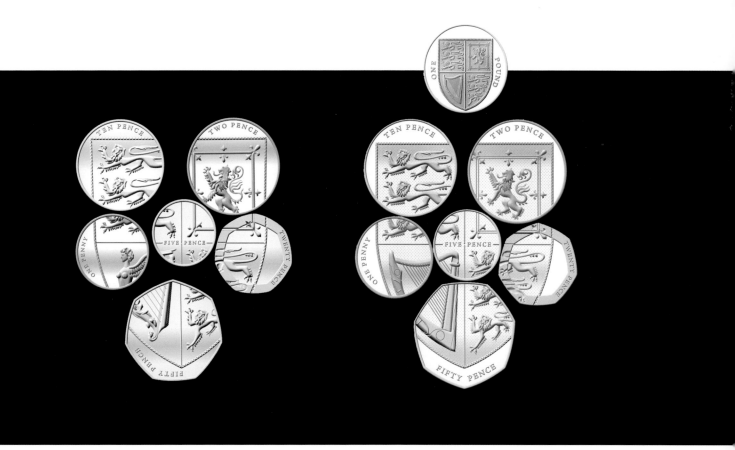

John Bergdahl, sculptor

My own involvement with this project began when, along with hundreds of others, I submitted designs in response to the Royal Mint competition to find new reverses for our coin of the realm.

Although my own efforts did not make the final selection, the quality of my work was good enough to attract the attention of Kevin Clancy, who deduced from the sculptural style of my drawings that I may have had previous experience of coin production.

I have in fact been both engraver and sculptor for some 45 years. After supplying the Royal Mint with samples of my work demonstrating my ability, it was decided to bring me on board to work with one of the short-listed artists whose designs had been selected for further development. The artist in question was Matt Dent whose imaginative and original concept was the eventual winner. Matt's background is in graphic design, so he produced his coin designs as computer renderings. As he had no previous experience of coin manufacture, my 40-odd-years' involvement with the industry allowed me to advise and guide him as to where minor adjustments to the design could facilitate the minting process. Fortunately he proved very amenable and understanding, and between us we were soon able to create a set of working plaster models to put before the Committee for further consideration.

The process was not entirely straightforward, several meetings were arranged between Matt, Kevin and me in order to review work in progress. Finally Matt called upon me in my Midlands home, with his girlfriend Diana, to give his final approval.

You will know by now that Matt's designs went on to claim overall victory in the competition, and I feel both honoured and proud to have been allowed to contribute and play my part in the process.

73

The plasters were approximately 1000% bigger than the intended size of the coins, making the five pence model about the size of a CD and the fifty pence model about the size of a dinner plate. Working on them at this enlarged size enabled John to incorporate significantly more detail.

As a trial, these plasters were scanned in to a computer, scaled down to actual size, and fed through a machine that engraves directly into metal. This gave us the first idea of the designs at their intended size in their intended material.

It was a heart-in-the-mouth moment to see how they looked as I gather that they either tend to work or they do not; there is always the chance that the amount of detail can become overwhelming and your eye finds it hard to distinguish one thing from another. A gorgeous eight-inch plaster model does not necessarily mean a gorgeous trial coin. On seeing them I was delighted with how they had turned out, and it really brought home the significance of the competition's outcome – I was not refining objects on a computer screen or discussing the finer points of a plaster model, I was holding a set of trial coins in my hand.

By this point there was one other set of designs remaining in the competition, by David Gentleman. I knew of his mural at London's Charing Cross Underground station but subsequently discovered the broad range of his interests and skills; a library of travel books illustrated in watercolour drawings, stamps and indeed two United Kingdom coins.

Strangely enough, as I have learned after the competition, his designs (although of different subject matter) like mine had an order, a sequence. His sequence was determined by the development of an oak tree, beginning as an acorn on the penny, maturing to a majestic tree by the fifty pence. Each design was supported by the elegant typography of the coin's denomination and framed by the border of the coin. The crisp lines of the design together with the simplicity of the sans-serif typeface gave the set a clean, bold approach. A lovely series.

Opposite: Scanning the plaster model for the two pence coin.

David Gentleman RDI, artist and designer

Definitive coins remain in circulation for a long time, so I set out to design a set that would wear well – coins that would be clear, interesting, striking and worth looking at more than once – with above all a theme appropriate to an intelligent and undeferential twenty-first century. Heraldic imagery, however time-honoured on the coinage, seemed to me to have become archaic and no longer relevant. Instead, I chose something actual, real, living, growing and beautiful: the oak, effectively our national tree.

The oak has always stood for strength and endurance: the Navy's 'wooden walls' are part of our heritage. Now, equally and importantly, the oak has acquired renewed significance in symbolising our intense new concern for nature and ecology – even, in a threatened environment, for survival. As cradled acorn, swelling bud, shapely leaf, the oak made a fascinating and varied theme; as sapling, in mature splendour and in majestic wintry silhouette, it also offered vivid national icons.

Matthew Bonaccorsi, Chief Engraver at the Royal Mint

It is an unfortunate reality of the Royal Mint's business that producing a coin can remove some of the subtlety of the original idea. If a coin design does lose any of its character, it is more often than not in the translation from sketch to sculpture. Matt Dent presented us with a well thought through idea, which had to be developed from a two-dimensional rendering to three-dimensional reality. Alongside the aesthetic changes made during the long journey from Matt's original, through two versions of plaster sculptures, digital models and finally to sample coins, we also had to juggle some serious technical challenges. The Royal Mint is a high-volume manufacturer, producing thousands of coins from each of its presses every hour. Creating the sculptures that will appear on those coins involves achieving the balance between aesthetic integrity and manufacturing efficiency.

Most of the new coin designs we make for the United Kingdom are commemorative, with production runs limited to a period of around one year. The old United Kingdom reverse designs have been a fixture in our factory for 40 years, adapting to changes in the production environment. So our challenge was not easy – take designs that have had four decades to 'run-in', and replace them with something we have never attempted before, do so discreetly, and in less than a year.

Although the process of making a coin is always the same, every new product is bespoke. The tooling is created specifically for the design, and how that design affects the movement of metal during the striking process. Matt's designs presented us with issues that were going to require some careful thought – the relief covered over half the surface area, and ran right to the edge of the coin, the last place that the metal in the blank discs of metal from which coins are made moves during striking. This meant that achieving the correct sculptural height in these areas would be crucial to avoid the risk of excessive tonnages when striking.

Not only did the design run to the edge, but that design was, in places, constructed of straight lines and sharp points – most notably on the border that formed the outer edge of the shield. This could cause problems during striking, as metal would move along the lines of the design rather than out from the centre of the blank. The force of the moving metal on reaching the weak area at the corner of the shield could crack the tooling.

Most of these problems were identified at the design stage, but there was one issue that did not come to light until we were well into the process of sculpting the models. The tooling for each coin in the United Kingdom currency is designed independently, with the relief height determined by the thickness and alloy of the blank used. When Matt's designs were scaled to fit the technical requirements of the blanks we noticed a vast difference in the appearance of the design on each denomination – especially between the five pence and fifty pence. The lines of the shield also looked different between one coin and the next. All six sculptures therefore had to be 'balanced' across the denominations, getting the most out of the blank, but also accounting for the change in relief scale on the adjacent coins. In order to make this process easier, we re-engineered the obverse effigy for each denomination. It was a time-consuming process but essential to secure coins that would strike correctly in the factory.

The task of creating this tooling went to our most experienced engraver, Robert Evans, who worked closely with Matt and the sculptor John Bergdahl. It is to his credit that, aside from some predictable fine tuning, these tools are performing almost as well as the previous designs. Production trial runs of the circulating versions have been particularly successful, and the resulting coins do justice to Matt's original designs.

Ahead of the final decision by the Advisory Committee there were further adjustments to the design, and a second set of plaster models was produced. This second set included a one pound model. Although this was not in the original brief, the Committee felt that the addition of a coin featuring the Shield of the Royal Arms in its entirety would help depict, define and support the entire design. An inspired idea.

The momentous meeting at which either a decision would be made on the winning series of designs, or all the designs would be scrapped and the Royal Mint would go back to the drawing board, took place on 14 March 2007. A bit of a nervy day that one, but a day which I will remember. It was a relief when the call eventually came and I was delighted to tell the good news to my family who had been closely following the development of my design from the outset of the competition.

There were still some remaining hurdles to clear at this point in the form of the approval of Gordon Brown (the then Chancellor of the Exchequer) and Her Majesty The Queen. I am delighted to say that both approvals were given.

I had been involved at all stages of the process so far, but I was not off the hook yet; the designer of a coin has not completed his or her task until the coin is struck. To have the business end of the Royal Mint's work revealed to me was both fascinating and deafening; hundreds of coin-shaped discs a second punched from sheets of metal, processed by thousands of moving mechanical parts, creating coins to be distributed in their millions. But there they were; the final coins, the finished article, the delightful and shiny result of the new reverses competition.

Above: The Royal Proclamation giving legal currency to the new coin designs.
Opposite: High-relief portrait of the Queen by Ian Rank-Broadley used on official medals and certain United Kingdom coins.

The visual language of coins

Stephen Raw

As the Royal Mint Advisory Committee's lettering 'voice' for the past three years, I have had the privilege of seeing Matt Dent's designs from initial line drawings right through to finished coins. Here are a few reflections on the nature of letters (and numbers) with which Matt and others are faced when submitting and progressing designs for the coinage.

When a designer has to choose a letterform for a coin there are a number of considerations and possibilities of which he or she has to be aware. I use the word 'letterform' here to signify that the letters might not be created from a computer font — they could be calligraphic or drawn by hand in other ways. Computer-generated fonts are very much the 'new kids on the block' in the history of coin design. Until recently coin designers had been responsible for making all the required letters from scratch.

One of the considerations is naturally legibility. Another is whether or not there might be an element of historical reference which could enhance a design. This could have the effect of making the letters less legible but, on the other hand, more in keeping with the period or other features of the design.

There are more than a few examples of this balancing act to be found on coins made by the Royal Mint. This gold crown (*opposite*) by Rod Kelly celebrating the 450th anniversary of the accession to the throne of Elizabeth I uses, as a reference, a contemporary calligraphic hand. Elizabeth was well known for being an advocate of 'Roman' lettering as opposed to the medieval letterforms still prevalent at the time. Rod Kelly's design is using appropriate letterforms rather than the most legible letterform available. After all, the words on a coin are not road signs – they are not required to be read at speed on a motorway!

ELIS
ATHENS
PARIS
St LOUIS
LONDON

IN
COMMEMORATION
OF THE OLYMPIC
GAMES HELD
IN LONDON
1908

B. MACKENNAL

The London Olympic centenary coin *(opposite bottom)*, designed
by Thomas T Docherty, uses as a reference the medals struck for
the Olympic Games of 1908. Even some of the letterforms' quirky
characteristics were employed on the new coin, for example,
the curly 'C'. The letters are treated in a modern and imaginative
way to enhance the strong feeling of perspective.

The historic archive of coins has been a rich seam for designers to mine. For designs he prepared for the British coinage in the 1920s, Eric Gill, the letter cutter and type designer, looked back at medieval coins which used the strong design of a long cross *(above)*. His careful drawings, kept in the Royal Mint Museum, show Gill's skill as a draughtsman – a necessary quality required of an artist even today when demonstrating the merits of their design *(left)*.

Gill's proposals were produced as trial coins *(above and right)* but whether or not his word breaks would get through nowadays is open to question. The tri-arch design on the threepence works particularly well; the letters and raised dots complementing one another *(above)*. His designs, however, were never adopted.

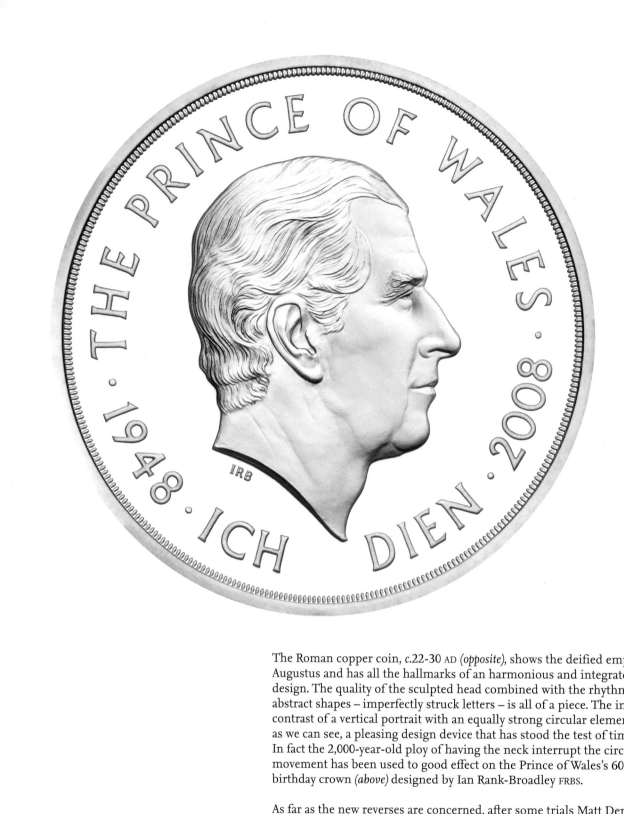

The Roman copper coin, *c.*22-30 AD *(opposite)*, shows the deified emperor Augustus and has all the hallmarks of an harmonious and integrated design. The quality of the sculpted head combined with the rhythm of those abstract shapes – imperfectly struck letters – is all of a piece. The inherent contrast of a vertical portrait with an equally strong circular element is, as we can see, a pleasing design device that has stood the test of time. In fact the 2,000-year-old ploy of having the neck interrupt the circular movement has been used to good effect on the Prince of Wales's 60th birthday crown *(above)* designed by Ian Rank-Broadley FRBS.

As far as the new reverses are concerned, after some trials Matt Dent eventually chose a bold weight of the Baskerville font *(sample shown below, letters in black are some of those which appear on the coins)*. It was a good choice for four reasons: it had the right amount of historical presence when used alongside heraldry; the letters were quite legible; the thick and thin strokes reflected well the quality of line used in the heraldic elements of the design; and it satisfied the demands of the manufacturing process – it is no good choosing a letter style that will not strike well.

BASKERVILLE BOLD

The choice of a font is always just the beginning of the process
– as Matt discovered. Fonts, until recently called typefaces because
they were coupled to the printing industry, are letters, signs and
punctuation designed to be repeatedly accessed; today this is largely
achieved by means of a keyboard. The clever part of any skilful text
font, as with the one these words are set in, is to make all the letters
fit well with any other letter that might come before or after it. An 'e'
has to work equally well alongside a curvy 's' or a geometric 'x'. In
the centuries before printing came on the scene a calligrapher made
each letter individually and could easily accommodate the preceding
and following letters.

The very nature of the reading process requires that letters are very
familiar to us. It is not surprising, then, how we can forget that letters
are just abstract shapes run one after the other in our system of making
language visible. When we remember this, however, it is easier to see
that words are simply *images*. If we can see them as such, they become
one of the pictorial elements in a design. When these elements combine
in an integrated way, an harmonious design can be achieved. Such
harmony can be seen on coins down the ages – it is by no means
a new phenomenon.

EACH CHILD BORN be NAMED WITH LOVE FOR EACH CHILD'S NAME A STAR ABOVE SO Let my name Be KNOWN O Let my Given Name BE KNOWN

Sometimes it is easier to appreciate that letters are images when the writing system is unfamiliar. Looking at this eighteenth-century Iranian silver coin *(opposite above)*, I do not need to know what the Persian says to know that it is a wonderful celebration of Arabic calligraphic forms. The stippled background within the spaces throws the organic shapes of these images into a delightful relief.

The illustration *(opposite left)* reproduces my pencil drawings for a forthcoming medal to be released through the British Art Medal Society. This personal style also celebrates the imagery and organic nature of letterforms unfettered from the strictures of a font. After being accepted, this original drawing was then outlined into a computer software programme *(opposite right)*, but the trick was to make sure it did not become too perfect!

The text is from *Rapture,* a T.S. Eliot Prize-winning collection by the poet Carol Ann Duffy, with whom I have worked on a number of projects. The painting shown *(above)* illustrates *Each Child's Name,* one of her Manchester Carols, which appeared in an exhibition accompanying their first performance at the Royal Northern College of Music in December 2007.

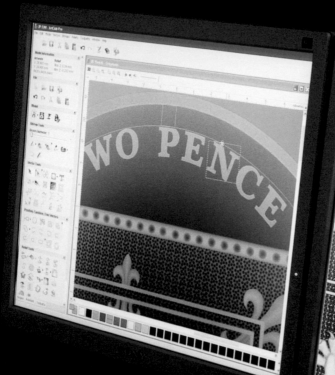

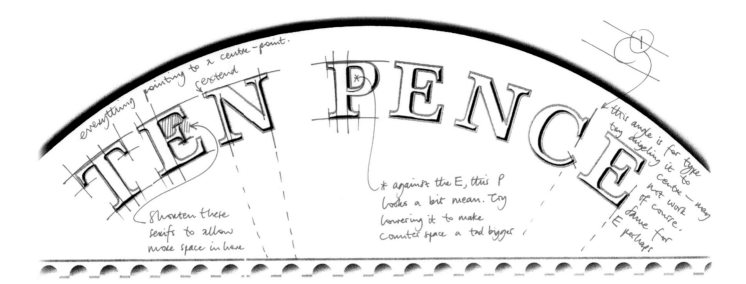

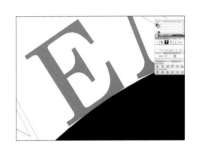

Predictably, text fonts are designed to work on a straight line. However, when curved, the spacing between letters does odd things, makes odd shapes. Not only this, but the letters themselves – designed to work on a straight line – are now fighting the very circular feel that a designer requires. The illustration of the letter E *(right)* demonstrates how a straight letter is unable to work on a curve. The black, solid letter shows how much work there is to do in 'editing' letters to begin to make them work in the round. The red outline is the original letter shape provided by the font.

Matt took on the challenge to examine every single letter in its particular context in a thorough and exemplary fashion. With notes I offered, alongside vital input from the Royal Mint's Engraving Team, Matt's hard work paid dividends, achieving that overall benchmark harmony. Some have asked why bother with such small detail which might well not be visible to the naked eye at the actual size of a coin. I proffer that the reasons are twofold – one visible, one not. The visible reason is that most new coins are seen at many times their actual size in printed and related publicity material, especially when launched. At these enlarged sizes there is nowhere to hide poor craftsmanship. The other reason is that there is an important quality issue at stake. Standards of good design and manufacture should be mindfully guarded. The Royal Mint is an institution that over the centuries has inherently demanded a high numismatic standard which continues to be recognised the world over. One might argue that if they do not care, who will?

Nevertheless, simply concentrating on detail is never enough to realise a good design. In Matt Dent's case his coin designs were a strong concept from the outset and they have been augmented as a result of getting all the elements working well together. In my opinion, the new reverses are examples of good numismatic design because they are graphically strong, demonstrating good contrasts within each coin; fresh – without being new for the sake of it; sculpted deftly; and superbly manufactured. The added value of individual coins being a part of a greater whole is just that: 'added value'. As they become familiar to the public, I venture to say that it will not be possible to handle any coin on its own without subconsciously knowing it relates to others. But for that theory to be tested we will have to wait a few years yet.

Receiving change:
reaction to the new designs

Kevin Clancy

One of the considerations faced by those who would seek to design a coin was encapsulated by David Gentleman in his beautifully observed book *Design in miniature*: 'Coins are both the most ancient form of design in miniature, and the most generally-used today. They are such common objects that one hardly spares them a glance, or pauses to consider whether a coin is well- or ill-designed – or even designed at all'. In August 2005 the Royal Mint embarked upon a wholesale process of redesign, which in part was aimed at encouraging people to look at the coinage with fresh eyes and to awaken an interest in these commonly used objects. On the eve of the launch of the new designs in April 2008, however, there was no way of knowing quite how they would be received and it was into this theatre of uncertainty that the Royal Mint stepped, together with the young graphic designer Matt Dent.

For those who had been involved in the two-and-a-half-year project to redesign the coinage there was indeed a certain amount of apprehension. People care deeply about what David Gentleman has called these 'fascinating and rewarding objects' and so understandably there was an earnest hope that the designs would be well received. But after all the carefully laid preparations, what if there were a leak or, of more immediate concern, what of the prospect of the disappearance of Britannia?

Opposite: Sestertius of Antoninus Pius (138-61 AD) showing Britannia.
Above: Penny Black postage stamp, first issued in 1840.

In late January 2008 an article appeared in *The Mail on Sunday* revealing that Britannia was to be removed from Britain's coins for the first time in over 300 years as part of the prospective change to the coinage. The story was picked up by some other national newspapers and over the course of a week people learned a great deal about the origins of Britannia: from her Roman incarnations, through her revival during the reign of Charles II, to compositional battles Christopher Ironside had with her at his home when designing the decimal coins. Frances Stuart, a mistress of Charles II who is widely regarded as having been the model for the Britannia on copper coins issued from 1672, was suddenly a cover girl 300 years after her death – the sort of fate, had there been an extensive tabloid print media in Restoration England, that might have befallen her at the time for her liaisons with the King. A campaign was mounted to save Britannia, a petition was handed in to 10 Downing Street and some MPs signed up to an Early Day Motion urging that she be retained on the coinage.

Britannia's presence in the seventeenth century was from the start intended as a symbol of British naval and military strength and she has since become both more and less militaristic in response to the politics of the time. A couple of decades after her appearance on halfpennies and farthings she found employment in another role as the symbol of the newly established Bank of England – within a generation she had become the mythical embodiment of the nation for international and domestic consumption and an emblem of financial stability.

The story in a more dilute form was to run for another two or three weeks but, whatever people's feelings for Britannia may or may not have been, there was a strong undercurrent of apprehension running through the episode concerning the actual devices that had been chosen. The frustration of officials lay in not being able to correct some of the wilder predictions of what was to appear on the new coins and in the few weeks before the unveiling the justification behind why Britannia would not form part of the series had, like the designs themselves, to be kept under wraps.

Above: Halfpenny of Charles II, 1672.
Opposite: Portrait of Frances Stuart, Duchess of Richmond by Sir Peter Lely.

The launch took place on the morning of 2 April at the Tower of London. Having been located there for over 500 years, the Royal Mint regards the Tower as its spiritual home and co-operation between the two organisations on exhibitions in recent years has reinforced a long-standing relationship. The unveiling of the coins was attended by print and broadcast journalists from national newspapers and television stations, as well as writers for design magazines and specialist numismatic publications. Professor Sir Christopher Frayling (Chairman of the Royal Mint Advisory Committee), Andrew Stafford (Deputy Master of the Royal Mint) and Matt Dent each made presentations, while Dave Knight (Director of Commemorative Coin at the Royal Mint) acted as master of ceremonies. Radio and television news and current affairs programmes covered the story, and the vox-pop reaction of people on the street, as well as the asides from television presenters, suggested a very positive initial reaction. At a reception in the Tower later that day the response was again favourable but what would the newspapers make of it all in the morning? To see the designs on the front page of *The Times* the following day was indeed gratifying. All the national papers covered the story in some detail, with editorials, too, remarking on the new designs.

Opposite: Enlarged replicas of the new reverse designs on display at the Tower of London.

Andrew Stafford, Deputy Master and Chief Executive of the Royal Mint

We had to make sure that the coin designs were true to the heritage of British coinage and gave fresh inspiration and modernity to it. I am delighted with the new coins which have been beautifully designed. They are contemporary yet retain the *gravitas* and reference to history required for the United Kingdom's coins.

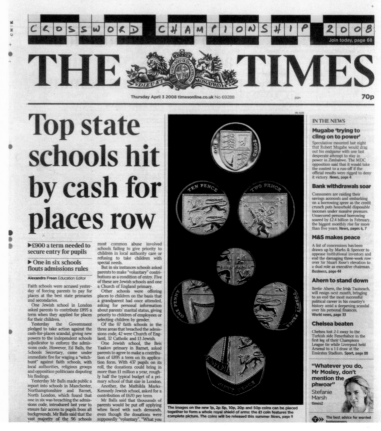

98

New coins for the United Kingdom

George III guinea

FIFTY PENCE

TWENTY PENCE

TWO PENCE

The £35,000 payday for a young man who had designs on money since age of eight

Hannah Fletcher

Matthew Dent with his new design for the £1 coin. It has the royal coat of arms on one side and the other the Queen's head

Matthew Dent was 8 when he fell in love with coins. It was 1990 and his friend brought a recently introduced 5p into school. "It was shiny and I wanted one," said Mr Dent. "It just looked amazing." Now, the 26-year-old graphic designer has been announced as the creative force behind the first new British coin series since decimalisation in 1971.

The vision for the coins beat more than 4,000 entries in a 2005 Royal Mint competition to find fresh designs for seven of Britain's eight circulating coins, from the 1p piece to the £1 coin. The £2 will remain unchanged.

All change

● In 2006 the island nation of Vanuatu released a limited edition series of coins in the shapes of various tropical fish
● Zambia created a series of coins to commemorate the Sydney Olympics in 2000 in the shape of the conjoined maps of Australia and Zambia, featuring the Queen's head and Sydney Opera House and the Zambian coat of arms
● To commemorate the 50th anniversary of rock'n'roll in 2004 Somalia issued a series of guitar coins, in the shapes of Gibson Flying Vs and those used by Gary Glitter and Abba
● Last year, using the latest in coin technology, Mongolia released a talking coin. While one side bears the Hongdaoi coat of arms, the other side has a picture of John F. Kennedy which declares: "Ich bin ein Berliner"
● Cook Island is working on coins featuring pieces of meteorites. One contains the Brenham Pallasite Meteorite, found in 1882 in Kansas

TIMES ONLINE
Inspired or infuriating?
Post your coin comments

Mark Brown
Arts correspondent

It's goodbye from Britannia and farewell from the crowned lion, thistle, plumed ostrich feathers and portcullis. Yesterday the Royal Mint revealed the first new coin designs for 40 years, dreamt up by a 26-year-old trainee graphic designer.

Matthew Dent, from Bangor, north Wales, who threw years ago was backpacking around New Zealand and Australia, beat of hundreds of other designers to win a competition to design the tails side of all British coins apart from the £2 coin.

The new design featured on the tails side of 50p coins from this summer

---

Britannia banished as coins get a makeover

By Martin Hickman
Consumer Affairs Correspondent

■ Heads or tails, history wins

Matthew Dent holds the £1 coin that shows the entire shield. Other coins, left, will show fragments

---

Picture gallery The new coins
telegraph.co.uk/pictures

Royal Mint unveils the new jigsaw coins

By Andrew Pierce

The coins, from 1p through to 50p, can be pieced together to form a jigsaw image of the royal coat of arms. The £1 coin, top, features the complete royal shield.

Editorial Comment: Page 23

COIN NEWS

incorporating BANKNOTE NEWS   MAY 2008

PRICE GUIDE
SHILLINGS, PLUS TEN POUND NOTES

A NEW ERA:
Britain's new coins unveiled

ISSN 0958-1391

THE NEW COINS' DESIGNER INTERVIEWED—SEE PAGE 28

BANKNOTE NEWS
Australia's $1 million dollar note

CLASSIS BRITANNICA
Roman Britannia ruled the waves

SCULPTOR EXTRAORDINAIRE
Designer of the world's most valuable coin

NEWS • FEATURES • NEW ISSUES • MARKET REPORT • VALUATIONS

All change for the coins in your pocket, as Welshman's designs are revealed

Tomos Livingstone
Political Editor

THE NEW POUND
Designer Matthew Dent from Bangor holds up the new £1 coin which shows the full royal coat of arms

Loose change

■ There are almost 28bn UK coins in circulation, with a total face value of more than £3.5bn;
■ If all the circulating coins were laid out side to side, they would form a line 397,289 miles long – 16 times the circumference of the earth;
■ The Mint can strike 14 coins per second on its up-to-date presses.

All Change!

Daily Mail, Thursday, April 3, 2008

Bye-bye, Britan... ...here is the ne... look for our co...

By Sam Greenhill

A VERY MODERN MAKEOVER

POUND COIN: Featuring the Queen's coat of arms, with the emblems of England, Scotland and Ireland

TEN PENCE: Three Lions of England

TWO PENCE: Lion of Scotland

ONE PENNY: Harp of Ireland/ Three Lions of England

TWENTY PENCE: Three Lions of England/Lion of Scotland

FIVE PENCE: (centre of card) Middle of shield on pound coin

FIFTY PENCE: Three Lions of England/ Harp of Ireland

'I can't wait to see people using them'

COIN WORLD

Besieged loyalists issue own money — See page 40

£1 coin celebrates 25th anniversary — See page 72

1943 Lin... elusive i...

This week in Coin World

APRIL 21, 2008

MINT SEES RISING BULLION SALES
Sales of all types of gold, silver, platinum coins up in March. See page 4

FED RESERVE MAY CUT COIN ORDERS
Inventory, forecasting ability may affect Fed orders from U.S. Mint. See page 4

YOUNG DESIGNER CREATES NEW LOOK
26-year-old may be the youngest designer of nation's coinage. See page 5

BRITISH MEDIA GIVE MIXED REVIEWS
Newspapers have much to say about the UK's new coin designs. See page 22

United Kingdom launches new coin de...
Seven coins share unified theme
BY JEFF STARCK COIN WORLD STAFF

No small change...

FIRST NEW DESIGNS FOR 40YRS OUT IN SUMMER

By Jake Morris

27 BILLION coins are in circulation...

REGAL: Britannia on the 50p, left, and on the silver bullion £2 coin, a collector's item not in circulation

Britannia may rule again...on £2 coins

By Rhodri Phillips and Simon McGee

BRITANNIA BANISHED FROM COINS

Man from the Royal Mint tells her in person: 'I'm sure you won't be made redundant'

---

design WEEK

News Analysis

Collect the whole set
They may retain some very traditional imagery, but the new reverse designs for UK coins feature a radical 'collective' idea, says Gina Lovett

FRESH FACE Mel Whitter, marketing manager at the Royal Mint with one of the new coins that were launched yesterday. Picture: Matt Fraser

COINING IT

Pack leader
...mpleton's animations

Picture: GEOFF CADDICK

FRESHLY MINTED: The £1 coin has the whole shield, and the 50p and 20p bear parts of its lower sections

JIGSAW PUZZLE: Two lions passant on the 10p, one rampant on the 2p, and odd bits on the 5p and 1p

It's bye buy to Britannia

By Tony Bonnici

THIS is the new look for our coins – and it's all change.

Britannia has disappeared after more than 300 years in our pockets, as has the portcullis and chains on our 1p pieces.

The new pound coin carries the royal shield of arms, and each lesser-value coin bears a different fraction of the image.

So the 50p piece has one-and-a-half lions passant plus the point of the Irish harp, the 20p shows just the hind quarters of the same lions, and the 2p has a lion rampant minus his toes. Only the £2 coin stays the same.

Britannia has been a fixture on our coins since 1672, but Gordon Brown gave permission for her to be removed in one of his last acts as Chancellor.

Philip Hammond, shadow chief secretary to the Treasury, said: "This is an act of wanton vandalism on our heritage."

The designs by Matthew Dent, 26, are the first overhaul for our coins since decimalisation in 1968. 'They come into circulation this summer, though the old coins will still be legal tender.

Royal Mint chief Andrew Stafford said they showed "fresh inspiration and modernity".

OPINION: PAGE 12

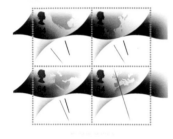

The idea of spreading a single design across a number of objects has had other expressions.
Top: Six book covers from a series designed for Penguin by Derek Birdsall.
Above: Millennium Timekeeper stamps by David Gentleman.
Opposite: Piero Fornasetti's *Adam* plates.

There was certainly criticism from the start in some of the main articles and particularly in the letters that followed. Papers whose own editorials had welcomed the series as 'handsome' subsequently published letters which took issue with the designs. In looking at the Media as a whole, however, the reception was overwhelmingly supportive of the change, a remarkable achievement indeed considering the sensitivity of releasing new definitive designs for the coinage. Phrases like 'clean, spare and logical', 'clever and enjoyable', 'ingenious' and 'innovative' were used and in the design community the series was more widely praised still for its clarity and boldness of conception. From this group more than most came the view that Matt Dent had responded to a difficult brief with imagination and flair. One design writer even went so far as to describe the designs as fantastic and astounding, their radical quality making them seem as if they were from a sleek, efficient, science fiction alternate universe version of Britain. Probably one of the least likely connections that could have been predicted was made between Enoch Powell's infamous Rivers of Blood speech and the new designs via the theme of social commentaries about Britishness. Then there was the religious angle. One letter compared Matt Dent's designs to *The Bible* in which many books, written over many years by many authors, form one brilliantly clever design.

In the days immediately following the unveiling a number of themes emerged, elaborated in letters to newspaper editors, to MPs and to the Royal Mint itself. Why was there no reference to Wales? Why had the 'English' version of the Royal Arms been used and not the Scottish? Why had the value not been included in numerals as well as words? Why was the coinage being used as a platform for post-modern art? And, inevitably, why had Britannia been dropped?

The question of Britannia had been raised at the press conference on the morning of the launch and it was explained that because all existing coins, including Britannia fifty pence pieces, were to remain in circulation, the symbolic figure would continue to be an active part of the coinage for many years to come. In addition, the prospect was by no means ruled out that she could well be the focus of future circulating coins. Whether it was these assurances, or the new designs themselves, the spotlight that had shone on Britannia gradually dimmed.

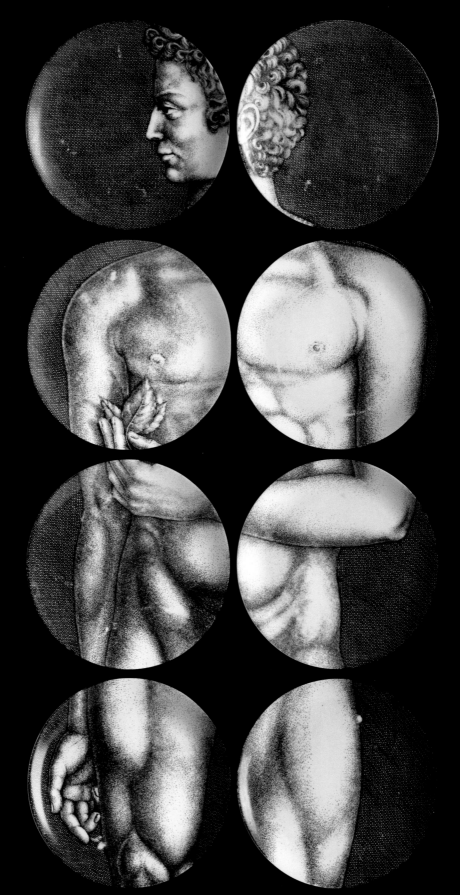

More generally, the reaction revealed how the release of the new coins was seized upon as a vehicle through which to make broader political points about the nature of the Union that is the United Kingdom. Historians and archaeologists often use coins as evidence in a similar way – treating them as documents of a particular time to support economic or political arguments, artistic or social comments. As potent symbols of a nation, coins have a habit of stirring up all the ways in which the roots of their meaning can be interpreted. The new designs were used in precisely this way – as a series of metaphors for aspects of national life about which commentators felt strongly. Political grievances bubbled to the surface focusing on the symbols used to represent Scotland, Wales and Northern Ireland and, as Clive Cheesman has noted earlier (pp18-19), the resolution of some of these concerns had been discussed at a senior official level on more than one occasion in the past. The validity or otherwise of the arguments will not be resolved in the pages of this book but once the prominence of news coverage surrounding the launch had died down the focus was directed elsewhere.

Mark Jones, Director of the Victoria & Albert Museum

No area of design touches more people more closely than designs for the coinage. Utterly un-remarked most of the time, occasionally pondered, they become enormously familiar and symbolically important. Few design problems can be harder than to encapsulate the United Kingdom's historic identities in a way that also reflects this country's present creativity and diversity. Matt Dent's designs draw on an historic symbol of national identity to create graphic images which are at once familiar and intriguing, unified and diverse, historic and contemporary. Classic and enduring, they also represent a very particular moment in the evolution of Britain's self-image and one from which future generations will construct meanings that we can only guess at today.

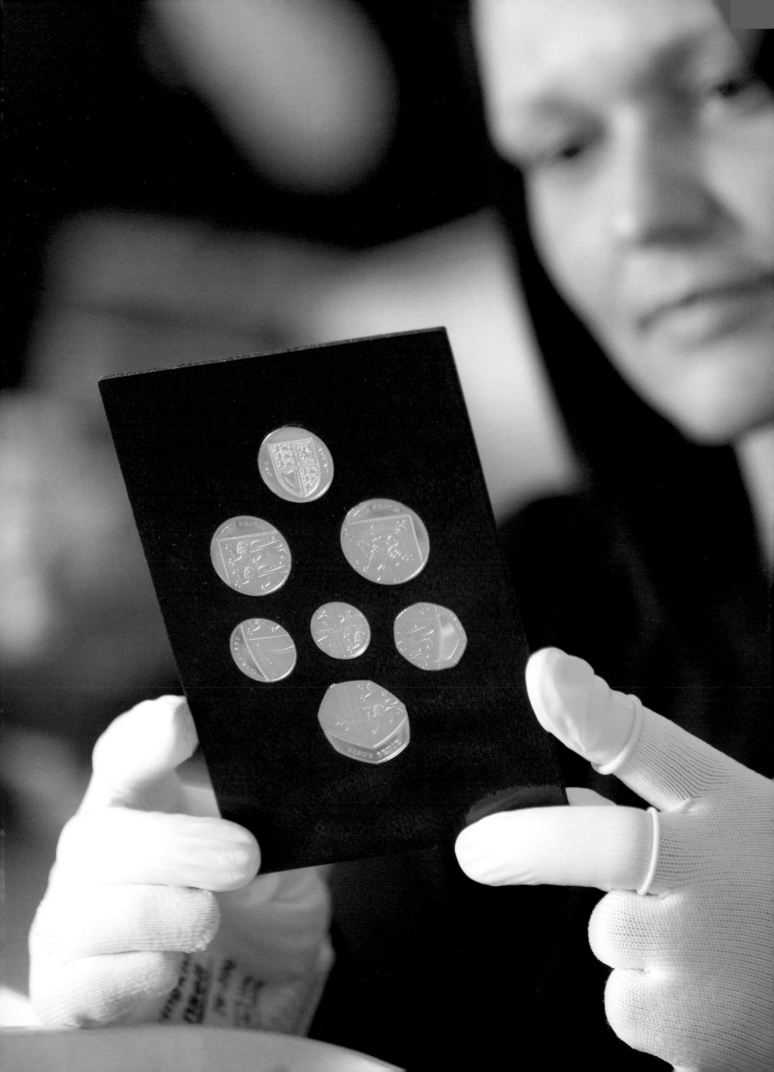

There was a further feature to the reaction which was particularly distinctive. No previous series of definitive designs for the United Kingdom coinage had ever been accompanied at their launch by their own blog sub-culture. Many hundreds, if not thousands, of responses to the new designs on all manner of websites sprang up and one has the feeling of only being able to skim the surface of what was actually out there. While the letters pages of national newspapers tended towards carrying opinions of a more critical nature, the website coverage offered a broader church of response. Defenders and opponents of the series argued their cases and that the new designs provoked such debate was itself of interest – for them to have been ignored would have been a worse fate than the comments of those who took issue with aspects of the change or indeed the need to make any change at all.

The commentaries on Matt Dent's designs have ranged from near conspiracy theory interpretations to considered praise. One of the strongest themes to emerge from the coverage on more than one occasion has been the sense of an ingenious concept, developed with the intensity and clarity necessary for successful coinage designs. Through them fragments of a whole are glimpsed, in a similar way to how other aspects of life are perceived, their contemporary cellular quality enhanced by the *gravitas* of their subject matter. In producing what is one of the most functional of objects and ubiquitous forms of art, the Royal Mint very often finds itself needing to balance all manner of interests and therein lies the challenge: the need to find a middle way and yet be bold, the wish to encourage people to spare more than a passing glance without being divisive. The positive impact of Matt Dent's series has revealed deeper aspects of their true merit, but what remains uncharted territory is how people will respond to carrying and using them every day.

notesfromtheblogosphere//sleeknewdesigns
innovativecontemporarywith*gravitas*and
historysmartmodernsimpleverycreative
antieurosentimentpleasingvariationexcellent
designsnonumeralsaproblemgoodvaluefor
moneywhychangeephemeraltootrendyavant
gardecleverplayfulfantasticdesignsastounding
respectfulmarriageofmodernityandancient
traditionwhereisScotlandhotdisapprovaland
conspiracytheoriesintelligentanti-Welshregret
lossofBritanniaprankmoderntakeonanoldlook
craftprettysharpnewdesignstheyaregoodfun
pleasantlysurprisedinterestingandunique
congratulatethejudgeseccentricpuzzlecoins
postmoderncleanandsparseadapteddeftly
willjointhemosticonicpiecesofartworkcan
telltheyweredesignedbyagraphicdesignerDent
hasdesignedcoinsthatmostpeoplewillprobably

Afterword

Alice Rawsthorn

Like most design critics, I tend to write about the striking stuff: things that are either so brilliantly designed that they deserve to be celebrated, or so dire that they are crying out for condemnation. What would you find more interesting? A design triumph that promises to make life easier and more enjoyable? A design disaster that does the opposite, but whose crimes deserve exposure? Or something so mediocre (and, sadly, most new designs fall into this category) that there is nothing much to say about it? Case closed.

Yet some of my favourite examples of design are not striking, but embody the quieter virtues of intelligence, elegance and simply seeming appropriate. I would be tempted to call them classic, if the word had not been abused so often that it has become design code for 'mediocrity'. So I will describe them instead as examples of 'quietly good' design, and they include the new United Kingdom coins.

These seven coins represented a doughty design challenge – summing up the spirit of a nation. How do you do it, especially if, like the United Kingdom, it is not really one nation, but an often uncomfortable collection of them? Matt Dent's response was to split the Shield of the Royal Arms into six fragments, and place one on the back of each of the fifty pence, twenty pence, ten pence, five pence, two pence and penny coins. Together those coins almost, but not quite, reconstruct the original shield, which appears intact on the one pound coin.

It is an inspired design solution. The ancient heraldic symbol is a respectful nod to tradition. Fragmenting it is a gracious acknowledgement of national differences with a fashionable whiff of deconstructivism. And it is all beautifully done. Thanks to digital technology, the metal can be cut more clearly and subtly than in the past, creating stronger contrasts of light and shade, which place Matt Dent's design in the modernist tradition of innovation.

Contributors

His Royal Highness The Duke of Edinburgh was President of the Royal Mint Advisory Committee from his appointment in 1952 until his retirement in 1999.

Clive Cheesman was formerly a Curator in the Department of Coins and Medals at the British Museum. He is the author of several works on coins and heraldry, and is currently Rouge Dragon Pursuivant at the College of Arms.

Dr Catherine Eagleton is Curator of Modern Money at the British Museum, having previously worked at the Science Museum, London. She has edited a comprehensive survey on the history of money and is currently working on a major project focusing on money in Africa.

Professor Sir Christopher Frayling is Rector of the Royal College of Art and Chairman of Arts Council England. He is well known as an historian, critic and award-winning broadcaster. He has published extensively on popular culture, design and the history of ideas. He has been Chairman of the Royal Mint Advisory Committee since 2000.

Dr Kevin Clancy is head of Historical Services at the Royal Mint and Secretary to the Royal Mint Advisory Committee. He has published articles and edited books on the history of the Royal Mint and the British coinage and is Director of the British Numismatic Society.

Matt Dent is a professional graphic designer based in London. He studied art at Coleg Menai in Bangor, North Wales and graphic design at the University of Brighton.

Stephen Raw is a lettering artist and a member of the Royal Mint Advisory Committee. He is a painter and designer of letterforms and has worked as a teacher and designer of book covers for many years.

Alice Rawsthorn is the design critic of the *International Herald Tribune*, and a columnist for the *New York Times Magazine*. She is also a board member of Arts Council England, and a trustee of the Whitechapel Gallery in London.

Acknowledgements

The Royal Mint would like to thank all the artists and designers who took part in the public competition in 2005 to find new reverse designs for the coinage.

The Royal Mint would also like to thank all those who have contributed to the preparation of this book, especially His Royal Highness The Duke of Edinburgh; Sir Christopher Frayling; the staff of the Department of Coins and Medals at the British Museum; Royal Armouries and Historic Royal Palaces (Tower of London); the British Postal Museum and Archive; the Fitzwilliam Museum; the College of Arms; the National Museum Wales; the Royal Collection and Ian Denyer at the House of Lords.

The Royal Mint gratefully acknowledges the permission granted to reproduce the copyright material in this book.

Every effort has been made to trace copyright holders and to obtain their permission for the use of copyright material. The publisher apologises for any errors or omissions in the list below and would be grateful if notified of any corrections that should be incorporated in future reprints or editions of this book.

All other images © Crown copyright 2008.

A frank and open relationship
p8 Seal of Alexander III (RH17/1/13) courtesy of the National Archives of Scotland.
p11 Gold seal of Henry VIII (PRO 30/26/35) courtesy of The National Archives.
pp12-19 Heraldic drawings courtesy of the College of Arms.
p19 Arms of Owain Glyn Dŵr courtesy of the National Museum Wales.

Christopher Ironside and the designs for the decimal coinage
Material from the Christopher Ironside archive
© Trustees of the British Museum.

Continuity through change
Sir Christopher Frayling's chapter is adapted from a lecture given to the British Numismatic Society in May 2008. He would like to thank Graham Dyer OBE and Kevin Clancy, for finding information and documents. The section on the Irish coinage is indebted to the illustrated book *Coinage of Saorstát Eireann 1928* (published in Dublin) and especially W.B. Yeats's essay 'What we did or tried to do', also to Roy Foster, *W.B. Yeats – the arch poet* (Oxford University Press, 2003). Above all, he would like to thank members of the Royal Mint Advisory Committee.
p63 Drawing courtesy of the Estate of Sir Hugh Casson.

Making an impression
pp68-69 Images from *Design Trends* © Matt Dent.
p75 Photograph courtesy of David Gentleman.

The visual language of coins
p83 Photograph of Stephen Raw courtesy of the *Manchester Evening News*.
p89 Copper coin minted at Rome, *c*.22-30 AD, showing the deified emperor Augustus © Trustees of the British Museum.
p90 Painting © Stephen Raw.
p91 Safavid coin of Shah Sultan Husayn of Iran © Trustees of the British Museum; medal designs © the British Art Medal Society.

Receiving change
p94 Sestertius of Antoninus Pius © Trustees of the British Museum.
p95 Penny Black courtesy of the British Postal Museum and Archive.
p96 Portrait of Frances Stuart, Duchess of Richmond, by Sir Peter Lely © The Royal Collection 2008 Her Majesty Queen Elizabeth II.
p98 Front page of *The Times*, 3 April 2008 © The Times/NI Syndication.
pp100-101 Articles from print media dated 3 April 2008 unless stated otherwise: Hannah Fletcher from *The Times* © The Times/NI Syndication; Mark Brown from *The Guardian* © Guardian News & Media Ltd 2008; cover of *Coin News*, May 2008 courtesy of Token Publishing Ltd; Sam Greenhill from the *Daily Mail* © Daily Mail; front page of *Coin World*, 21 April 2008, including article by Jeff Starck © 2008 reprinted by permission of Amos Press, Inc.; Jake Morris from the *Daily Mirror*, courtesy of Daily Mirror/Mirrorpix; Martin Hickman from *The Independent* © The Independent; Tomos Livingstone from the *Western Mail* courtesy of the Western Mail; cover, and article by Gina Lovett from *Design Week*, 10 April 2008 courtesy of Design Week; Rhodri Phillips and Simon McGee from *The Mail on Sunday*, 6 April 2008 © The Mail on Sunday; Andrew Pierce from *The Daily Telegraph* © Telegraph Media Group; Tony Bonnici from the *Daily Express* © Express Newspapers.
p102 Millennium stamps © Royal Mail; book covers courtesy of Derek Birdsall and Penguin Books.